L-D

THE GOD OF REASON

IS VOLUME

15

OF THE

Twentieth Century Encyclopedia of Catholicism

UNDER SECTION

I

KNOWLEDGE AND FAITH

IT IS ALSO THE

6TH

VOLUME IN ORDER OF PUBLICATION

THE TWENTIETH CENTURY ENCYCLOPEDIA OF CATHOLICISM

Edited by HENRI DANIEL-ROPS of the Académie Française

THE GOD OF REASON

By RÉGIS JOLIVET

Translated from the French by DOM MARK PONTIFEX

HAWTHORN BOOKS · PUBLISHERS · *New York*

First Edition, November, 1958
Second Printing, March, 1959
Third Printing, November, 1960

NIHIL OBSTAT

Hubertus Richards, S.T.L., L.S.S.

   Censor Deputatus

IMPRIMATUR

✠ Georgius L. Craven

   Epis Sebastopolis, Vicarius Generalis

Westmonasterii, die XI AUGUSTI MCMLVIII

The Library of Congress has catalogued this publication as follows:

Jolivet, Régis, 1891–
      The God of reason. Translated from the French by Mark Pontifex. [1st. ed.] New York, Hawthorn Books [1958]

      126 p. 21 cm. (The Twentieth century encyclopedia of Catholicism, v. 15. Section 1: Knowledge and faith)

      Translation of Le Dieu des philosophes et des savants.
      Bibliography: p. [127]

      ---

      1. God.   I. Title.   (Series: The Twentieth century encyclopedia of Catholicism, v. 15)

BT101.J613   231   58–11597

CONTENTS

INTRODUCTION   7

I. THE MORAL WAY   14

II. THE METAPHYSICAL WAY   32
    Can we demonstrate the existence of God?   33
    The metaphysical proofs   45

III. THE NATURE OF GOD   82
    The divine attributes   82
    Pantheism   90
    The divine personality   96
    Creation and providence   99

CONCLUSION   113
    The proof of God   114
    Atheism   118

SELECT BIBLIOGRAPHY   127

INTRODUCTION

At the root of all man's restlessness and all his philosophical speculations there is, I think, only one problem, namely, *the problem of God*. Does God exist, and, if he exists, what is his nature? There, surely, is the question of questions, to which all others lead and which it is impossible to escape. Not only is this so from the standpoint of philosophy, which inquires into first causes and first principles and cannot, therefore, abstract from the problem of God without denying its very purpose, but also from the more broadly human standpoint; our whole life is determined by the question. For the meaning we find in human existence must depend entirely upon the solution we give to the problem of the existence and the nature of God.

1. *Meaning of the term God*. We are asking whether God exists, and, if he exists, what he is. Clearly this implies that we already have some notion of God, for otherwise the inquiry will be impossible: we cannot inquire into something of which we have no knowledge whatever. The notion of God is, I hold with Descartes, that of a being "sovereign, eternal, infinite, unchangeable, all-knowing, almighty, creator of everything outside himself",[1] in short, that of an infinitely perfect Being, absolute cause of all that exists.

Now this notion is by no means held by all who use the word, God. It will be felt that there is little connection between the God of the Semangs of Malacca, the God of the Vedas, the God of Aristotle, the God of Spinoza, and the Christian God. Yet this objection need not delay us. For first, the philosophical or technical, as they may be called, concep-

[1] Descartes, *Third Meditation*.

tions of God are the result of a long process of abstract
thought and are found at the end, not at the beginning, of
the speculative inquiry, and, secondly, there is a notion of
God, more intuitive than rational, more synthetic than
analytic, which seems by far the most common and most
universally distributed over all the world and throughout the
ages, being closely linked with the different forms of religion
which divide humanity. It is this notion which I am suggest-
ing, whatever formulas may be used to bring out its meaning.
It is a notion so general that all philosophers must try to
make their definition conform to it. I shall start from this
definition of the term, and shall ask whether experience and
reason support it or disprove it.

2. *Reason and Revelation.* It is important to make clear
the precise question I am asking. Pascal, in a well-known
passage in his *Memorial,* speaks of "the God of philosophers
and scholars", and opposes this to the God of the Christian
Revelation, to "the God of Jesus Christ": that is the subject
we have to deal with. It should be noticed that this discussion
is limited to what can be known of God in the light of natural
reason alone, and therefore does not include what we learn
from Revelation, the mysteries of which (the Trinity, the
Incarnation, the Redemption) are beyond the reasoning
powers of any creature, and can only be known and believed
through faith, which is a free gift of God.

We must, however, clearly understand what this limitation
implies. Even though the light of faith cannot directly help
us in a purely rational inquiry, it can assist and clarify the
philosopher's work in the sphere of reason by the support it
gives *from outside.* Mystery is a source of light in the rational
order, careful though it is to preserve its rights and only
follow its own rules. "By this vivid appreciation of the divine
mystery—the God of Abraham, of Isaac, and of Jacob,"
writes Maurice Blondel, "is not the strictest philosopher
rightly prepared to accept, to realize in his thought and in
his life, the idea and the presence of that inviolable secret of

INTRODUCTION 9

a *Deus absconditus,* of a God whom we cannot reach unless he reveals something, however little, of himself, unless he communicates himself, unless out of his love he unites himself with us in order to raise beings other than himself to his own beatitude and friendship? The philosopher does not find in the thought of a living and transcendent Truth, which possesses itself and gives itself, a theory incapable of standing up to criticism; he can reconcile the God of Abraham and of the Gospel with the most stringent demands of reason."[1]

I need say no more about the relation between faith and reason, between philosophy and revelation, that is to say, on the question of Christian philosophy, as the subject will be dealt with in another volume of this series.

3. *The meaning of proof.* What is meant by proof in its most general sense? It means either to establish by means of experience (direct or indirect) the existence of a fact or a being (proof from experience), or else, by a process of reasoning and starting from certain premises, to reach a conclusion which follows necessarily from the premises (proof from reason). The essence of such a proof is to make (or show that there is) a necessary connection between two concepts. This is called a demonstration.

Now plainly there is no proof of God in the first sense. For God, if he exists, is not an object or a thing of which we have experience of a scientific type, and no such experience, that is, such as leads to a scientific proof, is possible. If God exists, he cannot be perceived by the senses. Hence, if there is a proof of God, it can only be a proof from reason; it can only take the form of a process of reasoning or of a demonstration, and can only be expressed as a necessary conclusion from this reasoning.

But I must explain more exactly the meaning of demonstration. This may be *a priori,* when it starts from the essence of a being or its essential properties (thus we demonstrate that

[1] M. Blondel, *Bulletin de la Société fr. de Philosophie* (séance du 24 mars 1924) (Paris, 1928), p. 55.

man is free because he is reasonable), or *a posteriori,* when it starts from effects given in experience (thus the fact of tides serves to prove the gravitational pull of the sun and moon). The first kind is seen in the ontological argument, the second is seen best in the traditional proofs, that is, the moral proofs (from moral duty, from the unchangeable principles of truth and good, and so on), and the metaphysical proofs (from change, efficient causality, contingency, final causality).

The *a posteriori* proofs of God, that is, those which proceed from the world to this first cause, have a unique character, which makes it impossible to equate them with demonstrations valid in the physical order (thus the example of the tides only applies roughly or analogically). For the term of the demonstration, God, remains always outside our grasp, beyond our power of experience: God appears as implied by what we know, but he is not grasped as an object of our experience. From this point of view he is an hypothesis, but a necessary hypothesis, without which nothing can be explained and everything becomes irrational. On the other hand the idea of God as such is, in a sense, previous to the demonstration, just as the hypothesis must precede the inductive process. The process of reasoning only serves to make explicit a sort of intuition, not of God in himself, but of the reasons which support the assertion of his existence. Hence it is that the explicit proofs often seem less strong and less satisfying than the intuition which lies behind them. For the intuition, being thoroughly synthetic in character, makes us not only aware of God as a spiritual presence (in Pascal's words: "God perceptible to the heart"), but also aware of ourselves as included and involved in him, while the analytic explanations tend, if we are not on our guard, to make God into an object of our experience and a concept. Thus we can see why the traditional proofs have so often met with resistance, for example, on the part of Pascal, or, in our own days, of such thinkers as Edouard Le Roy or Gabriel Marcel.

Again, however valid the proofs of God's existence may be

in themselves, absolutely speaking, they can only be valid *for us* in so far as we accept them on our side, with honesty, moral rectitude and purity of heart. The proofs are not compelling, as are proofs from experience. We can use an expression of Gabriel Marcel, and say that they are "ways of approach to the ontological mystery". That is undoubtedly why St Thomas called them *viæ*, ways or directions.

4. *General method*. These remarks show the main lines of the method we ought to follow. Thus it will be a *rational* method, since God, if he exists, of his very meaning, is not an object of experience. (Though we must make exception here of mystical experience, which will be considered later on.)

On the other hand the method will not be *a priori* and deductive. (Here, again, we must make exception of the ontological argument which we shall examine in due course.) For, first, we cannot ever deduce God (as a particular fact is deduced from a more general fact), since, of his very meaning, God, if he exists, is transcendent to all that exists and has nothing beyond him: he is not included in any genus (that is, he is not part of a greater being). And, secondly, every proof must start from our experience, since God, not being in himself an object of our experience, can only be known through his works. Hence the proof of God is based on reality, though it is never precisely a proof from experience. It is from within the being in which we are and which we are, that we shall try to find the evidence which God, as first cause and ultimate reason of all that is, gives of himself in our moral consciousness and our being. It follows that we can only know God in terms of being, and also that our method of inquiry, starting from being, demands nothing else whatever than acknowledgement of the implications involved in the very fact of the being presented to our experience.

5. *Plan*. The plan we shall follow will, then, result, according to usual custom, from the requirements of the subject. Theodicy—a word first used by Leibniz as title to his treatise in defence of divine justice against the objections drawn from

the existence of evil, and which later passed into common use to refer to the whole mass of questions concerned with the existence and nature of God—has three main divisions: (1) the existence of God; (2) the nature of God; (3) God's creative action.

Dealing with the first of these divisions we proceed from the concrete to the abstract. Theodicy in general appeals to what is called "pure reason", which is, of course, only an abstraction, and confronts this pure reason with a number of arguments which are called *metaphysical*. These arguments are strong ones, and it will be my task to explain them. This, however, I shall do later: I think it is better to adopt a more concrete and intuitive method, and to start with reality, psychological, moral and social.

The idea of God, as involved in the definition of the term given above, is reached through the family and society. It is further developed in our minds by a mass of deep intuitions, which show it to us as based on reason, and necessary to give meaning to life, to justify duty and moral obligation, and satisfy the demands of the heart, and so forth. Moreover, we cannot fail to come across, whether through the spiritual life or through study, those great mystical souls who have claimed to come into touch with God. Indeed it is no exaggeration to say that the idea of God confronts us on every side. Even the struggles in which we are involved, or those of which only the report reaches us—struggles which centre round the idea of God, such as the discussions of modern atheism—give to this idea additional importance and urgency.

Many men get no further than this, and are content to live the idea of God which has been passed on to them, and the practical value of which they have found by personal experience, but without analysing it. It will be our task, however, to go further, and to test what may be called the metaphysical content of belief in God. When we make an effort to reflect, we see displayed before the mind's eye one or other of the arguments called *metaphysical*, which are specially used by philosophers, and which pass from the world, considered under a particular aspect, to God. These proofs are so general that all men who believe in God have a kind of intuitive notion of them. They support our idea of God, and give it an objective basis. But, when elaborated in a scientific form, they are liable to appear abstract and difficult and for this reason I shall only discuss them at a later stage.

In the second part, devoted to the nature of God, I shall have to emphasize the "personality" of the divine being, and the insurmountable problems involved in any pantheistic conception. I shall add to this second part some remarks on the meaning of creation and on divine providence.

CHAPTER I

THE MORAL WAY

1. *The notion of a moral proof.* From the psychological point of view, which is that of most concrete experience, the moral way of coming to God is far the most common. Usually man comes to God under the pressure of the deepest demands of his heart. These demands are also rational demands, because they include a process of reasoning which leads to an acceptance of God's existence as the only adequate explanation of our moral experience. This reasoning, however, usually remains implicit, and the movement which leads to God rather takes the form of an intuition. Pascal speaks in this connection of the "heart" or the "feelings": "It is the heart," he says, "which feels God, and not the reason", and, "reason bases itself on the knowledge of the heart and on our instinctive knowledge, and these are the foundation of all its arguments." The word "intuition" must not be taken to mean here, as it does in its strict use, the immediate concrete apprehension of a reality existentially present to the knower, but only the general, synthetic, grasp, without explicit process of reasoning, of the rational grounds for a truth of the intelligible order, in this case, the truth of God's existence. Thus this intuition implies a whole process of reasoning, which the rational arguments only serve to analyse and make explicit. That is why we can say, with Le Roy, that, in the problem of God, "everything depends on the inner witness given by our moral consciousness", and, that "the true light comes from a deeper source than the sight of phenomena or the play of events: from our moral experience". Yet this view, which

is derived from St Augustine, must not lead us to depreciate
the value of the metaphysical proofs for God, but only to
realize that our moral experience, which introduces us to the
idea of God, includes in some sense every proof of God, and
gives a spiritual meaning to the metaphysical proofs, which
without it are apt to persuade us without touching our hearts.
In fact moral consciousness is an expression of the reason
itself, if taken in its fullest sense and widest range.

Thus understood, the moral proofs by no means tend to
make us reject the way of reasoning in order to come to God,
or to substitute for it a proof from experience as the only
ground for belief in God, since they themselves can only
receive their value and their force from the reasoning which
they necessarily include. The religious instinct and the heart
are indeed only different names for a single thing, namely
reason itself when it seeks an intelligible explanation of man
and of the world. It is from this point of view that I must
first explain them.

2. *The unchangeable principles of truth and goodness.* Man
is a restless being, because he is a thinking being. He finds
himself set in the midst of a universe immensely greater than
himself in space and time, and yet he aspires to know the
whole on which he depends. The very success of his attempt,
the gradual victory of science, shows him that his aspirations
are, at least partially, justified. The universe is intelligible; it
expresses order; it reveals a certain unity; it appears directed
towards ends. How can this be explained without God? How
can we assert that a universe which in some sense we can
possess by our thought, and which appears to us as a cosmic
thought, is not itself the result of a Thought? At once reason,
as a kind of intuition, feels that a rigorous choice is imposed
upon it: either God or sheer absurdity.

This choice becomes especially pressing when it is imposed
in the moral life. Has life any meaning? Our moral consciousness answers emphatically, yes. But may not this answer be
an illusion, the result of some remote social pressure or of

early training? This has been put forward as a theory, but it has not been proved. Moral requirements cannot be disregarded because, if we do not admit their absolute value, life will end in pure negation; our conduct will be without significance, for good and evil will be the same. Now the principles of justice, of truth, of goodness, lay an absolute obligation upon us, with the characteristics of universality and eternity, and must therefore be founded upon some absolute Truth and Goodness, a universal final end. Otherwise they will only have the strength and persistence which belong to our own thought, and the passing character of this is manifest. Thus moral values seem to demand God, and without God to be reduced to nothing.

3. *Moral duty.* Then, too, the idea of duty and the conditions under which it develops point inevitably towards God. For us to act is to strive and work in conformity with duty, with the demands of morality. Indeed it is to strive in two senses, because it is to overcome the resistance of the external world and the still more obstinate resistance of the internal world, in order to build in ourselves and around ourselves a spiritual order, which alone, when all is said, can give meaning to the unending struggle man carries on with himself and with the world.

We have a clear perception that everything, in ourselves and throughout the universe, has its purpose in a spiritual and moral order, which must result from our efforts and sacrifices. Man, weak and small in the midst of the cosmos, yet gives the universe its highest meaning, because by his reason he confers upon it a kind of intelligible actuality, and by his conduct he directs its powers towards their proper ends, both rational and spiritual.

But how could the mind, which dominates the universe, be nothing more than a product of this universe? The idea is clearly absurd. It would be equally absurd to suppose that the sense of duty which controls our thought and our conduct is only a result of vague, general, cosmic forces. In fact it is not below us that we must seek an explanation of our spiritual and moral powers, but above us, in a reality which has a richer being than the universe or than we ourselves. A. E. Taylor expresses this well in a recent book when he says, ". . . whole-hearted acceptance of the postulates of the moral life itself involves an outlook on the world and on man's place in it which is more than merely moralistic. The good man who thinks out to the end the implications of his loyalty to the moral good . . . will find that he is pledged to something more than simple recognition of an ideal of conduct as entitled to his unqualified respect. He is committed . . . to a belief in the final coincidence of the 'ought' and the 'is', in virtue of their common source in a transcendent living and personal Good—one, complete, eternal—the only belief which rightfully deserves to be called belief in God."[1]

4. *Man's destiny*. Undoubtedly, then, we have intuitions of this kind which give us a strong conviction that death cannot be our final end, a plunge into nothingness. Surrounded on all sides by miseries of every sort, some from the hostility or indifference of the elements, which science can indeed mitigate but cannot abolish, others, infinitely more distressing, from man's injustice, civil strife, social inequalities, or moral sufferings which no scientific remedy can heal, and finally from the pain of death, we feel instinctively that we can only find a sure refuge and full security in the protection of a just Providence, without which human life would be but a deception, in Shakespeare's words, "a tale told by an idiot, full of sound and fury". For, if there is a cosmic order, as science tells us on the evidence of the immutable laws it discovers, surely there is still better ground for thinking there is a moral order, an order clearly revealed by the unwritten laws invoked by Antigone in a famous passage of Sophocles, and deeply impressed in our hearts and moral consciousness? And if this moral order, which demands the triumph of good over the powers of evil and of injustice, of suffering and of death, is

[1] *The Faith of a Moralist* (London, 1930), II, p. 1.

not realized here below, are we not justified in believing there exists a Providence which regards the merits of the just man as well as the crimes of the wicked, in order to reestablish a spiritual and moral order, which the world seems incapable of enforcing? It is for these reasons that man, who never finds the full satisfaction of his aspirations here below, and in any case is faced in the end with the scandal of death, turns naturally to God, and in so doing affirms his belief in a sovereign and incorruptible justice.

Can it be said that there is anything irrational in this, that it is a mere movement of the heart which cold reason cannot guarantee? On the contrary, it is by the very exercise of reason, where it applies most certainly and most objectively, that we are forced to turn to God, and are justified in so doing. It may often happen, as I said above, that the process of reason remains implicit and obscure, and that our feelings can only fall back on their own needs for justification. But their way of acting is fundamentally so much in accord with reason itself that we find it used as an argument for the immortality of the soul and the existence of God in the most varied philosophical contexts, for example, in the *Phaedo* of Plato. "Therefore", says Socrates, "not only am I not distressed at dying, but I have good hope that there is something after death, and, according to the ancient belief, something better for the good than for the wicked."[1]

All the more weight is given to these arguments from the fact that our will, of itself and through its own movement, by a kind of immanent logic, turns towards the absolute Good and absolute Being. That is the subject of the great work of Maurice Blondel, *Action,* and it is bound up with the whole Augustinian tradition. "We cannot get away from what we wish for", writes Blondel, "even when we seem not to wish for it. The whole mystery of life rises from this superficial disagreement between the apparent desires and the sincere aspirations of our original will. Behind all human will there

[1] Plato, *Phaedo*, 63 C.

is a sort of rough sketch of being, which can never cease to be, but which, when not filled in, does more harm than if it did not exist. And, in order that this outline may be filled in, it must be perfected by a hand greater than that of any human being. Man can only win his being by renouncing it in some way, in order to bring it back to its origin and to its true end. . . . We must give all for all. Life has a divine reward, and, in spite of weaknesses of pride or sensuality, mankind is generous enough to attach itself all the more to him who demands more from it."[1]

Very often, no doubt, our actual conduct contradicts our deepest will, that will which is our nature. But frustration of our moral consciousness, hindrances and failures of every kind, constantly warn us of our mistakes and make us obey more faithfully the demands of our fundamental will to be. In this movement, as Blondel shows, it is impossible to stop: neither pleasure nor knowledge nor art can satisfy our aspirations which are infinite in scope. They carry us irresistibly beyond what is human, to God, the final end, in which alone our heart can find utter peace and joy. "Aspirations for the infinite", writes Le Roy, "constantly act upon us. They are more deeply rooted than desires on the surface of experience, and nothing in this world can ever satisfy them. Here below we are confined on every side; time swallows us up, and the being, in which we wish to dwell, escapes us. Is it possible that our all should consist in such misery? If so, nature, in making us live, would have set us moving towards nothing. Here we are faced with an intolerable riddle and we can never give up trying to solve it; to do so is an imperative need. You know how we have come to this. At the source of the restlessness which torments us, our deepest will is revealed to us, and at the centre of this, our moral needs. As answer to the creative movement which springs from these, comes a first faith, the breath of life of the spirit within us. Now, only God can explain this movement of such supreme significance.

[1] M. Blondel, *L'Action* (1893), p. 491.

Hence to live is to believe in God, and to know God is to become aware, by the very act of awareness, of that which lies behind the fact of living a human life."[1] Thus we realize how closely God is present to us. It is in ourselves, in the development of our whole will, that we grasp him, in the well-known words of St Augustine, as "closer to ourselves than ourselves, and above the highest that we possess". We have not, then, Maurice Blondel tells us, "to seek the necessary outside the contingent, as a further end". It is in the contingent itself that we apprehend it as a reality, present and actual, immanent at the very centre of all that is, for, in the words of St Paul, "in him we live, and move and are". At the same time we recognize that this final end, which is God, is beyond every end, beyond all being, since it is their explanation. This necessary Presence is also an absolute Transcendence, if it is true, as we shall see later on, that only the Transcendent can be really immanent in all.

5. *Objections against the moral proofs.* We must notice two difficulties, which are often brought forward. One is raised by the sociological school (Durkheim). It claims to explain moral obligation and the sense of duty by custom or heredity, resulting from the pressure of society upon the individual over a long period. First, we should notice that this theory, as we should expect from Durkheim, does not deny the need to reach a transcendent principle. I say that this transcendent principle is God; Durkheim thinks that it is simply society. Everything depends on the arguments by which he supports his case, and the essence of Durkheim's theory reduces itself to the questionable argument: morality is for the sake of society; therefore morality is derived from society. There are many defects in this reasoning, and I must briefly sum them up. First, it cannot be said that morality is for the sake of society, since society cannot be considered as the whole final end of morality: there are many moral duties

[1] Ed. Le Roy, *Le Problème de Dieu* (Paris, L'Artisan du livre, 1929), pp. 249–50.

which do not have as their end society as such, and which may sometimes even force us to oppose social demands. Secondly, it should be specially noted that we cannot deduce from the fact that society is the partial end of moral obligation that the whole force of the obligation comes from society alone, in other words, that society is its efficient cause. Indeed we know ourselves as human persons, as terms of moral obligation imposed not only on other persons, but on society itself. Hence from this point of view society appears as subordinate to the human person, that is to say, to the moral and spiritual values which define humanity. Again, society acts by compulsion. But nothing is more opposed to moral obligation, for this requires in the subject internal liberty together with understanding of the law, and respect for the lawgiver. Durkheim, of course, maintained that social compulsion would be gradually rendered more internal, and transformed into moral obligation. This argument, however, is not based on facts, and plainly presupposes the solution it offers. Hence we need not discuss it; it is not so much a proof as the simple assertion in other terms of the sociological theory.

Another objection consists in accusing the moral proof of begging the question. It is claimed that by explaining moral consciousness as a consciousness of obligation, the notion of supreme lawgiver is assumed, while the proof professes to deduce it by a process of reason. My reply is that this objection bears witness to a virtual and confused knowledge of the existence of a lawgiver as implied in the sense of moral obligation. But to say this is not to beg the question, since, as I have been careful to show, this confused knowledge is fully explained by the very reasons which the argument only serves to make explicit by a discursive process. The assertion of the existence of God as first principle of the moral order, as supreme lawgiver and universal Providence, is thus not a mere assumption. It is nothing else than the metaphysical interpretation of the fact which defines essentially the moral consciousness, and also the making explicit of the reasoning by which this consciousness turns spontaneously towards the transcendent Good, living and personal, which alone can explain what it is.

6. *General consent.* The argument based by long tradition on the general consent of the human race, throughout the world and throughout the ages, in affirming the existence of God, can be connected with the moral proofs. Thus I must explain it and examine it here.

Reduced to its simplest form this argument consists in an appeal to the facts of the general belief in God, in order to draw the conclusion that this belief answers to an absolute demand of the human spirit, and consequently cannot be false. The Stoics and Cicero in early times were fond of developing it, and French traditionalists (Lamennais, de Maistre, de Bonald) repeated it in a more systematic form. They maintained that the problem of certitude, as it concerns fundamental truths, cannot be finally solved on the level of individual reason, for this, left to itself, is exposed to a fatal scepticism; it can only be solved on the level of the general reason, or of "general consent", that is, of tradition. The existence of God, says Lamennais, is shown by the evidence we find in the universal consent of peoples, and this evidence has such force that we cannot reject it without also rejecting reason, and all that gives value to human life and cohesion to the social organism. The existence of God is thus one of those basic and fundamental truths which are previous to all demonstration.

To appreciate this argument at its true worth, we must examine it on two points, namely, the fact of general consent, and the value of this fact as a proof. Now, in the first place, it can be disputed whether there is general consent, for, if in every age there have been atheists, even though they have been a minority, this is enough to take away the absolute value claimed for the argument. Moreover, even if we admit the fact of general consent, it is not, of itself and by itself alone, a proof of truth, since the general agreement of minds can sometimes be explained by the existence of accidental causes which produce errors, impossible to detect and remove. We know that for many centuries the human race universally agreed that the sun went round the earth, and that the earth was the centre of the universe. Again, contrary to the opinion of the traditionalists, no certitude is valid unless justified by reason or experience: without this an assertion is never more than an opinion, however widespread it may be.

Nevertheless the appeal to general consent, so far as it applies to the existence of God, is not deprived of all value. For, if this consent is not universal, it is so widespread and constant in the human race, throughout all the varied and dramatic changes of its history, it has resisted and still resists so many obstacles which again and again stand in its way, that we cannot deny that it corresponds to a demand of reason. At the very least it implies that the idea of an absolute seems native to the human mind. Only sceptics reject this idea, and they do so in word alone. For when rejected in theory, it reappears, even among atheists, or those who call themselves atheists, in one form or another. Progress, or History, for example, are secularized absolutes which take the place and the value of the absent God. In Russia, especially among the younger generation brought up in the official atheism, we can see quite plainly how the need of religion is changed into the cult of the regime and its myths, new rites being substituted for those of the traditional religions.

I may add that, if we are to give a true estimate of the general belief in God, we ought not to underrate or simply dismiss its popular forms which are sometimes rather vague, nor even the crude forms assumed by belief in God among peoples we call primitive. For it is true that religion cannot dispense with imagination, and Descartes himself, following Aristotle and St Thomas, remarks: "Just as the imagination uses representations to conceive of bodies, so the understanding makes use of certain sensible objects, such as breath or light, to represent spiritual beings."[1] But the imagination which serves the reason is itself religious, however badly it expresses itself. It seems indeed that the stories about the divinity in which it intervenes anthropomorphically in history, have been themselves inspired by an effort of thought which seeks to explain particular things and the universe at large. If the writing of stories, even to express the truth, tends to make God into a man, and so to make him a character in history, the true spiritual idea of God, still recognizable in the stories about God's action in the world, lies at the root of the development of myths. The very effort, which we see revealed in ordinary expressions, to purify our ideas and terms as much as possible from contamination with the sensible, shows clearly that even in uncultured and primitive man there is a tendency towards more correct expression of the experience which he has of himself and of the world's meaning. It is one of the great illusions of the sociological theory of Durkheim to want to explain everything by the "primitive", whereas the latter is hidden and confused, and, in order to yield its true meaning, requires a gradual process of explanation by means of a long historical inquiry. We *think* what the primitive man *felt* (for he thought badly), and indeed, though we think better than he did, we often *feel* less keenly. In fact we only make actual what was in potency in his experience of life, for his experience was ill served by grossly inadequate concepts.

From this point of view philosophers have no advantage over the man of common sense. Subject like him to the inevitable deficiencies of language, and, in spite of themselves, exposed to the unfortunate ambiguities of analogy, they have tried to translate into more or less accurate concepts the deep sense of godhead which man has always had. Very often, however, their conceptualizations have turned out to be a long way from corresponding to the truth and the fullness of feeling and the intensity of living experience. In fact this

[1] Descartes, *Olympica* (*Œuvres*, Adam-Tannery, x, p. 217).

experience tends to become rather a religion, a personal
relation with the Godhead, than a simple metaphysical affirmation of God. Perhaps, indeed, when all is said, the simple
imagination in certain expressions of popular belief is richer
and more vigorous than the learned discourses of philosophy.
For what matters is the lively sense of metaphysical demands
in being, as given in experience, and philosophy only has
value in so far as it harmonizes its theories with these essential
demands.

7. *Mystical experience.* The problem of God is also raised
for the philosopher's consideration by the mystical experiences of which the great monotheistic religions offer us so
many examples. Great religious souls have asserted that they
have experienced contact with God in a manner inexpressible
in human language, but such as to reveal directly the presence
of God. Of course illusion may be suggested. But we must
realize all the difficulties involved in this explanation, when
it applies to sound and sensible minds, characters utterly
upright and sincere, persons whose lives have been so fruitful
in good. We shall surely be wise to listen to what they tell us.

Illusion, then, is insufficient as an explanation, but, even
if illusion is present, it will still have to be shown how all the
facts of mystical experience and all mystical experience itself
can be adequately accounted for by a purely natural explanation. Such an explanation has been attempted by certain
philosophers (among others, Janet, Leuba, H. Delacroix).
Starting from the inner mechanism of mystical states they
have tried to show how, through the working of this
mechanism alone, we can explain all the phenomena which
the mystics regard as supernatural, and as revealing a transcendent God who illuminates their minds without employing
the normal processes of intellectual life. The psychologists
of whom I speak will tell us that there may be a revelation,
but it is only a revelation of the subconscious, which, in
virtue of a psychological automatism, suddenly rises to the

surface of consciousness, and then gives the feeling that it is an activity from without which has manifested itself.

This is the theory defended in particular by H. Delacroix, though with moderation and subtlety. "The feeling of passivity", he says, "which is so strongly expressed by the mystics, and makes them think they have reached a transcendent state, and are in touch with a higher activity, the action of God, is due to ignorance of what happens within themselves, of their subconscious activity. They feel that their will does not cause these states, because they seem to come of themselves." Hence they must be attributed to an abnormal cause, because, according to the mystics, these states "have a value, a content and a power, beyond that of nature", while nature cannot exceed itself. Delacroix adds: "The hypothesis of a subconscious activity, supported by certain natural dispositions and governed by a controlling mechanism, exactly takes the place of the alleged external cause, and fully explains this feeling of passivity and of otherness. . . . The subconscious here consists in the fact that the germs prepared by the reflective consciousness, falling upon a nature ready to receive them, mature and blossom without the subject observing any of this process. He sees only the beginning and the end, and, since he does not observe what comes between them, he does not understand his own productive powers."[1]

Nevertheless, this interpretation, though following a method which professes to keep close to the order of nature, is—whatever Delacroix may think—far from explaining the facts it sets out to explain. We must not, of course, substitute a supernaturalist for the naturalist *a priori*. But we must be ready, if the facts demand it, to pass beyond the purely natural order, and to conclude that God is really present to the soul of the mystic. Now it should be noticed how the passage quoted from Delacroix gives a verbal solution, in which the problem is regarded as solved by an explanation

[1] H. Delacroix, *Les Grands Mystiques chrétiens* (Paris, 1938), p. 405.

which in fact is only an hypothesis, and needs to be proved instead of being itself at once accepted. The thing to be proved must not be turned arbitrarily into the proof itself. On these lines the psychological automatism of the mystic ought in principle to explain everything. But since obviously it is not sufficient, they add a "methodical determinism" or a "mechanism" which, "supported by the moral tension of asceticism and of interior liberty", help to produce "those high states which seem supernatural". And, as "the moral tension of asceticism" has never been found capable, by itself, of producing a mystic, we are told of "an innate aptitude for intuition". In other words they go on to grant precisely what is in question. It is in the same way that the divine is made to emerge from the subconscious or unconscious, by putting it there from the beginning under the form of "dynamic automatism" and "creative subjectivity", expressions which describe the problem, but do not supply any solution. Moreover, the appeal to "psychological mechanism" would leave the problem of God's existence untouched, because why and how this mechanism was supposed to produce belief in God would be left unexplained. Merely to assert that this results is again nothing else than to assume what has to be proved. In short these conclusions are not reached by a strict analysis of the psychological data, but by a naturalist philosophy which altogether rejects *a priori* the supernatural or divine in its true sense. Whatever they may appear on the surface, these methods of approach are not scientific.

Many arguments, too, encourage us to believe the mystics when they claim to have come into touch with God. For the mystics tell us that they communicate with a being who is living, and a person, in a supreme sense. They speak with God. Now this disproves the theory of a simple subconscious activity, since we know that the further we get from the living centre of consciousness to go down into those regions of consciousness which are obscure and then completely dark, the further we get from that which is personal, to enter into the impersonal. We should also notice what a depth of thought is implied in these experiences of the mystics. In their writings they try in stuttering words to convey something of what they have learnt when raised in ecstasy, and they make us believe them. Many of them have entirely lacked the previous theological training which could explain their enlightenment. Such for instance is the case with Marie de l'Incarnation, who wrote in a letter to her son, Dom Claude Martin (October 1671): "I can assure you that before this happened I had never been instructed in this great and adorable mystery. And even though I had read and re-read it, the lesson or instruction given by man could never have impressed me as I was then impressed and still am." But what she said in these words when she received a revelation regarding the Trinity, all mystics could say. Unless, then, it is due to a real experience of God, how can we explain the wonderful increase in depth, clarity and precision which the mystics receive from their visions and ecstasies? Again, is not Baruzzi right in saying that "contemplation is a form of knowledge in contrast with the false apprehensions with which men are usually satisfied"?[1]

Finally, the moral effects of these visions, the spiritual vigour which mystic souls receive from them to undertake and carry through resolutely the noblest and most difficult works, disprove the theory of pure illusion. This is sufficiently shown from the false mystics whose lack of fruitfulness is so characteristic. To interpret as divine action what was only autosuggestion or an obscure form of automatism would lead to madness, and not to the heights to which true mystics are raised. Bergson has seen this clearly, and expressed it in a fine passage. "There is", he writes, "such a thing as intellectual health, firmly established and exceptional, which we can recognize without difficulty. It shows itself in desire for

[1] Baruzzi, *Saint Jean de la Croix et le problème de l'expérience mystique* (Paris, 1924).

action, the ability to adapt oneself to fresh circumstances, strength combined with subtlety, the prophet's perception of what is possible and what is not possible, and also common sense of the highest kind. Is it not precisely this which we find in the mystics of whom we are speaking (that is, the Christian mystics)? Could they not help us to define what intellectual health really means?"[1]

In view of these arguments must we not admit that mystical phenomena reveal God, in some such way as the description given by a traveller reveals that a country exists, though we cannot go there? We are faced with an experience of the divine which cannot adequately be explained unless we suppose God exists, and this experience is seen at its highest in the Christian mystics. Of course a mystic can be mistaken, but it would be inconceivable, indeed impossible, that all should be deceived, and deceive us when they tell us, with such force and conviction, of the supernatural realities which they have known from direct personal experience, and which cannot be communicated to others. We understand how Bergson could write, after speaking of the agreement with which Christian mystics describe their experiences, that in this we see "the sign of an identity of intuition, which can be explained most simply by the real existence of the Being with which they believe themselves in communication".[2]

Yet, in spite of all this, we should not be justified in finding here a proof in the absolutely strict sense. For we cannot base a proof on mystical experience, even granting it unanimous, unless we have already reached the existence of a personal God by another way, either by that of the moral proofs discussed above, or by that of metaphysical reasoning, which we shall next discuss. It is clear, however—this was also Bergson's opinion[3]—that the witness of the great Christian mystics, of itself and through its own evidential

[1] H. Bergson, *Les Deux Sources de la Morale et de la Religion*, pp. 243–4.
[2] H. Bergson, *ibid.*, p. 265.
[3] H. Bergson, *ibid.*, p. 265.

value, renders probable in a high degree that the transcendent personal reality exists with which they claim to have been in contact. This witness plainly supports and confirms all that we learn about God and his nature by faith and by reason.

8. *Concluding remarks about the moral proofs.* All these facts, then, moral, psychological and social, as well as mystical experience and the almost universal belief of mankind, prevent us from regarding the problem of God's existence as unreal and force us to think of it as real and inevitable. But, still more, to the extent I have indicated, they lead us to conclude that there is no solution to this vital problem except by belief in a personal God, who is infinite Knowledge and Love.

Yet the arguments I have put forward are not the only ones: there are others, more abstract in character, at least apparently so, but which must influence strongly all who follow reason. These other arguments lead us to the same conclusions as the first, but they do not start from the realities within our consciousness, as do the moral proofs strictly so called with which we have been dealing, and which are based essentially on the moral experience of the human consciousness. These further proofs are those called metaphysical, and I shall go on to discuss them.

CHAPTER II

THE METAPHYSICAL WAY

We do not enter into an entirely new region with the metaphysical proofs. Throughout the previous discussion we have
had to use metaphysical principles on which to base the
reasoning. Indeed, in one sense every proof of God is metaphysical, so far as it seeks to establish the existence of a
Being, who is, as the definition implies, beyond the sensible.
Nevertheless, if we wish to classify the proofs of God in
accordance with their starting points, the division into moral
and metaphysical is justified. This will be all the clearer if
we speak here, not so much of metaphysical proofs as of
physical (or cosmological) proofs, because henceforth we shall
take as our basis physical facts, or, if you like, things and the
properties of things. We shall start from objective reality as
definite as movement or becoming, causality, contingency,[1]
and the purposes found in nature. However, I am retaining
the expression "metaphysical proofs", in order to avoid the
danger of misunderstanding which might ensue from speaking
of "physical proofs". This might be misinterpreted, and easily
suggest the idea of a demonstration of the same type as that
used in natural science. Moreover, I wish to emphasize that
all the proofs of God only receive their form, and can only
be understood, by reference to the demands made on the
reason by being, that is, by reference to metaphysics.

All these new arguments, then, clearly resemble the fore-

[1] Contingency (from *contingere*, to happen) is the characteristic of
all that is conceived as capable of either being or not being. Thus
contingency is opposed to necessity of being.

going, in so far as they are based on experience. Experience is the only ultimate ground for demonstration. The proofs of God are subject to this law, and the existence of God can only be shown by an *a posteriori* demonstration, that is, one which starts from beings and concrete facts, physical or moral, perceived by experience, and which passes from them to a real Being, without which these beings and these facts and the whole universe remain unexplained and inexplicable.

Objections of principle have been raised against the metaphysical proofs, and these objections may be classified in two groups which are the exact opposite of one another. The first includes the objections which aim at showing that any proof of God is either impossible or self-contradictory. The second group, on the other hand, asserts that the metaphysical arguments are useless, because the existence of God is, of itself, a truth so evident and necessary, that it is necessarily incapable of demonstration, the only possible proof of God consisting in reflection on our consciousness of the general evidence. We must, then, carefully examine these two classes of objection.

I. CAN WE DEMONSTRATE THE EXISTENCE OF GOD?

We have to deal here with four kinds of argument. In order to make them clear I must give some account of them, and shall sum them up under the names of Emmanuel Kant, Léon Brunschvicg, Edouard Le Roy and Jean-Paul Sartre. Only the last of these professes a strict atheism. Brunschvicg defends a spiritualism in which God is the name for transcendent, impersonal Reason. On the other hand Kant and Le Roy both acknowledge the existence of God, but do not believe we can accept the metaphysical way without errors of reasoning. To them the moral way alone seems valid, though there is an essential difference between Kant and Le Roy. Kant thinks that moral reality is only capable of leading us to belief in God as a postulate of duty, that is, on the ground that the moral life demands it, though this cannot be rationally demonstrated. Le Roy thinks that the assertion of God's existence rests wholly and only ("the only perspective", he writes, "which is valid without limit or reason")[1] on our grasp of moral reality and our perception of its implications, and that this experience, when correctly interpreted, is capable of forming the basis for the soundest and most invincible of arguments.

1. *Kant*. The essence of Kant's objection consists in denying that we can validly employ the principle of causality to reach the transcendent, that is, to pass beyond the sensible world. As all the metaphysical proofs for God rest on this principle, since they aim at showing that God is the cause of the universe, these proofs would thus be rendered valueless, and would only show the demands of our minds' structure, but not objective demands, in the strict sense. "If, in fact", writes Kant, "only objects of sense can be our data, and if they can only be this in the context of a possible existence, it follows that nothing is an object for *us* unless we suppose the whole of empirical reality as condition of its possibility. But, by a natural illusion, we extend to all things in general a principle which, properly, only has validity relatively to those things which are given as objects of our sense", and we make of this the transcendent principle of the possibility of things in general.

To discuss this objection thoroughly we should first have to criticize the very principle on which it is based, and which lies at the root of the whole of Kant's system. That would take us too far afield. But the criticism can be put briefly by saying that Kant's error, when he makes his universal denial that reason can ever pass beyond the phenomenal order, results from the empiricist postulate which assumes that knowledge can only reach the sensible. In fact we can see that these two propositions are the same, and Kant's sophism lies

---

[1] Ed. Le Roy, *Le Problème de Dieu* (Paris, L'Artisan du livre, 1929), p. 249.

in professing to prove the first by means of the second, of which it is only another form. Again, when Kant asserts that all causal series which appear to us in phenomena are derived from the *a priori* forms of sensibility and understanding, and that the metaphysical proofs of the existence of God are merely paralogisms of pure reason ("all speculative knowledge of the reason", he writes, "reduces itself to objects of experience"), in fact he only repeats, without proving it, the empiricist postulate of his whole system. But this postulate, which implies that we can only have an intuition of the sensible, is so open to criticism that in fact the great majority of philosophers, from Plato and Aristotle, Augustine and Thomas Aquinas, to Descartes and Malebranche, Bergson and Lavelle, reject it. As against the opinion held by the author of the *Critique of Pure Reason,* in agreement with the empiricists, they make it clear that we are capable of intellectual intuition, that is, that our thought has the power to grasp being in the sensible, the eternal in the temporal, the absolute and necessary in the relative and contingent, and that it is nothing else than this power which renders metaphysics possible and legitimate.

Kant's hypothesis, moreover, involves in itself sufficient difficulties to put it out of court. The chief of these lies in the impossibility of explaining the irrational element, whether apparent or real, with which our minds so often come in conflict in the scientific or philosophic examination of the universe. If, as Kant supposed, "nature is entirely the work of the mind", it is impossible to see why nature presents the mind with riddles and mysteries. This difficulty becomes greater with the progress of science.

2. *L. Brunschvicg.* We must now consider another aspect of Kant's theory, which has often been put forward by modern thinkers. They bring against the proof for God's existence the accusation that it is based on an unproved postulate, namely, that reason can transcend the order of sensible experience, and thus that in reality it merely begs the question.

These thinkers criticize the theory of analogy which controls the whole field of theodicy. As this line of argument has been developed with much force by Léon Brunschvicg (1868-1944), following Kant, I shall refer to the principles of his philosophy and, as this brings us to the very essence of the metaphysical proof for God, I shall consider it in some detail.

First I will quote Brunschvicg's own words. He tells us that all the traditional arguments to prove the existence of God are based on an alleged ontological causality. The world would be an immediate datum for us "with its movement, its causality, its contingency, its hierarchic structure, its finality, qualities for which you claim complete intelligibility. But all these qualities, which are inherent for you in the reality such as you give it to yourself, are to the modern mind, on every rational ground, mere appearances due to the play of the imagination. Your alleged need of intelligibility amounts to treating the problems of nature as if they were not problems of nature. You think that the world is a work of art; you claim there is an artist, although the psychology of this artist, whether he fashions or creates the world, has always resisted every attempt to make it intelligible. It is very difficult to see in this anything else than a postulate derived from an outworn anthropomorphism."[1]

To this argument of Brunschvicg I reply that the statement that movement, causality, final purpose, are only appearances due to the play of our ontological imagination is very much open to debate. The opposite would appear, rather, to follow, if it is true that the notions of being, cause, end, movement, as well as the first principles of being, are ultimate notions, perceived intuitively from the first contact of mind with experience. It seems undoubtedly true that these notions are in no way accessible to the imagination, but refer to intelligible realities and necessities, because they imply relations which only the understanding is capable of conceiving. On

[1] L. Brunschvicg, *Bulletin de la Société fr. de Philosophie* (1928), p. 71.

the other hand are these realities of the physical world, movement, causality, final purpose, intelligible of themselves? Does the universe possess in itself the sufficient and ultimate reason of its being? That is the problem we have to face, and it cannot be avoided.[1] We may wish to treat the problems of nature as problems of nature. But manifestly to declare *a priori* that nature itself as such is not a problem amounts to absolute refusal of speculative research, so that it is only seen as a mere postulate, the very theory we have denounced above in Kant. Existing things can be quite well explained up to a certain point without going beyond nature. Phenomena and the qualities of the universe can be looked at as intelligible in a certain degree by establishing, by scientific knowledge, their mutual relations. But this explanation and this kind of knowledge remain superficial. They do not get to the root of the problem of being, or of movement, or of the hierarchic structure of the universe, or of its complex unity. They tell us *how,* but not *why.* They explain the nature of a thing, but not its being. That is why, after having analysed and explained nature as nature, we have further to explain it as being and as existence, and this explanation is, strictly speaking, metaphysical.

Brunschvicg, however, does not think this answer is conclusive, and, like J. Lachelier, believes it contains a paralogism. For, he says, if it is true that every effect supposes a cause, this cause is necessarily of the same order as the effect. Hence, once again no transcendent use of the principle of causality is possible, and thus it follows *a priori* that any attempt to prove the existence of God falls to the ground.[2]

Here we find once more, but under a slightly different form, the Kantian critique. Even so it does not seem to me to be sound. It should be noticed that, if it is affirmed *a priori* that

[1] Cf. J. Lachelier, leçon xv, *Cours de logique,* quoted by G. Seailles, *La Philosophie de J. Lachelier* (1920), p. 129.
[2] Cf. Brunschvicg, *Le Progrès de la conscience dans la philosophie occidentale* (Paris, 1927), p. 114; *La raison et la religion* (Paris, 1939), pp. 40 et seq.

cause and effect can only be expressed univocally, this at once plainly begs the question—the very offence of which the proofs for God are accused. It is precisely the question whether they are univocal which we have to discuss, and to decide this from the beginning is to abandon the problem, and also to propose an indefensible argument. For, when we speak of cause, clearly we do so in reference to being, that is to say, in so far as causality is the act of making being real. Consequently the difficulty is involved in being, and consists, as Brunschvicg puts it, in saying that we can never get beyond the being of *nature*. But this difficulty is met if we remember that being is seen first as a transcendental, that is, as a notion applicable universally to all that is or can be, and hence as an analogical notion.[1] On what grounds, then, can it be said to be impossible to apply this transcendental, analogical, notion —which of itself implies freedom from any limitation—to an infinite being? To deny that it can be applied is to assert *a priori* what is in question. Now, what I have just said about being must be repeated in exactly the same sense about the notion of cause, or the principle which makes being real. Like the notion of being it can apply to every kind of being without any restriction. It can be used analogically and apply to an infinite and transcendent being, if the argument leads to this. Finally, every finite being, being multiple and in a state of becoming, must be contingent, and necessarily demands an actualizing cause which is itself pure act, essentially one and unchangeable. It demands this, as I have shown above, not if we go back in time, but here and now, for each contingent being, as well as for the contingent universe itself.

Yet this is still not enough in Brunschvicg's view to justify the metaphysical proof for God's existence. "With the best will in the world", he says, "I cannot close my eyes to the fundamental confusion between two types of analogy which have scarcely anything in common but the name. Analogy is

[1] I deal more explicitly with the notions of contingency and analogy in Chapter III.

either, honestly and exactly, the precisely defined proportion between measurable terms, hence belonging to the same type of experience or thought, or it is only proportion in a metaphorical sense, and the metaphor is then a sin against truth. It is a relation invented, by means of the extrapolation that language allows, between terms of which one at least would have to be regarded as outside all human experience and all true human thought. If from the invention of this relation we conclude to the discovery of the term, we find ourselves looking at our own hypothesis. To compare the world to a clock is to have already invented the clockmaker. The so-called reasoning of Voltaire[1] is rendered no more valid if you suppose that the clockmaker himself created the material he needed. All this, for modern thought, seems to me to be obvious."[2]

The question of analogy, raised here by Brunschvicg, is certainly complex and difficult, and has occasioned keen controversy. I think, however, that the answer can be confined to some clear and certain points. Brunschvicg says that analogy can only be valid if it refers to terms of the same type of thought and experience. But that is the whole question. It seems more true to say that, by definition, there cannot be analogy between terms of exactly the same type, that is to say, terms which refer to things of the same genus or species, nor indeed between terms which refer to quite different kinds of thing. Otherwise we should contradict the most genuine modes of thought and even of being. The attraction which an end exercises, and the impulse given by an agent are plainly not entirely alike. Nevertheless we use the same word, causality, to refer to both of them, because, in spite of these

[1] Cf. Voltaire, letter to the Marquis de Villevieille, August 26th, 1768: "The atheists have never answered the difficulty that a clock proves a clockmaker." Elsewhere Voltaire writes: "The universe puzzles me; I cannot imagine how the clock can go, and yet there be no clockmaker."

[2] L. Brunschvicg, *Bulletin de la Société fr. de Philosophie* (1928), p. 63.

actions being essentially different, we see that they both have
a positive part to play in the constitution and modification of
things. In this respect we call them analogous. I think it is
impossible to rebut this evidence. Why, then, should not the
creature and God, natures essentially different, have this in
common analogically, this likeness, that each of them, each
in its own way, is something which formally excludes not-
being? And why, when we grasp both the creature and God
under this precise aspect, should we not pass from the one to
the other, and, starting from the one, make a valid inference
to the other? When he opposes this process of reasoning, as
when he denies its power to give knowledge, Brunschvicg
comes up against the firmest of reality, and the most natural
of logic. If the problem of analogy in fact amounts to nothing
else than the problem of the validity of a relation between
terms which are neither precisely the same nor completely
different, when Brunschvicg maintains there is nothing
between pure homogeneity (or univocity) and pure hetero-
geneity (or equivocity), he only asserts *a priori* the very
matter which is in question.

We can, then, I think, at least conclude from this discussion
that no decisive argument has been raised against the validity
of the proof for God, and that the objections we have been
examining rest in fact on principles without rational support.

3. *Edouard Le Roy*. One of the points on which Le Roy
has most insisted in his criticism of the metaphysical proofs
for the existence of God is that the universe appears as an
indivisible whole, and that all dividing up of this universe
into individual beings and distinct things is a fiction invented
by the discursive intelligence owing to need for action. It is
just this fiction, thinks Le Roy, which leads us to look for
causes of phenomena. Yet, if we agree that the world forms
a whole, the totality of the phenomena is explained adequately
by reference to the whole, and thus we have not in any sense
to look outside the universe in order to find a cause, for
which, in fact, it has no need.[1]

[1] Cf. Ed. Le Roy, *Le Problème de Dieu*, p. 93.

The weak point in this objection is pretty clear and I need not dwell on it at length. First, we can quite well admit the unity of the whole without feeling obliged to deny the reality of distinct beings and things within the whole. Their reality impresses itself on us in the clearest way, at least so far as biological individuality is concerned, and all the more in regard to individual human beings who are directly aware of existing in themselves and for themselves, as independent and autonomous. Secondly, if it is true, as Le Roy asserts, that within the whole the phenomena and the beings which appear distinct only owe their consistency to their being correlative and to their reciprocal causality, and hence if it is true that they can only be explained by reference to the whole, it follows that the totality of these phenomena or of these beings which individually lack reality, cannot have more consistency or reality than the individual phenomena of which they are made up. Here again we cannot explain the whole by itself, and say it is its own cause. It must necessarily be conceived as independent, in its being and in its activity, upon a cause which is higher than it, and essentially distinct from it.

At this point Le Roy puts forward a difficulty which shows clearly that his argument is unsound. "The problem of the first cause", he writes, "is not really the true question. Science indeed, does not solve it, nor seek to do so. It asks under what conditions and as a result of what inherent necessity phenomena work themselves out. That is all."[1] Certainly this is so if we are only concerned with science in the purely positive sense of the word. For science of its very meaning in that sense, being only knowledge of the laws of the sensible world, cannot pass beyond the universe: it is entirely enclosed in it. But it is quite another matter with philosophic thought and metaphysical reasoning. To confine their scope to that of the positive disciplines would be to return to the old positivism and the naturalism of which, nevertheless, and quite rightly, Le Roy wishes to hear no more.

[1] Ed. Le Roy, *ibid.*, p. 35.

But let us leave aside what may be regarded, in Le Roy, as an inconsistency, and let us examine the deeper sense which he intends to give to his objection. "The whole", he writes, "does not present itself as a system open to deduction, that is to say as a closed and static totality, given to us once for all. It is, rather, an act of causality in actual process. We see, then, why we cannot say that it has a cause."[1] In fact, adds Le Roy, the term, causality, can only be given two senses, neither of which can validly lead us to God. It means, on the one hand, logical dependence, and, on the other, creative activity. Consequently the idea of cause tends ultimately to be equivalent either to the notion of mathematical identity or to that of free will. Now in neither of these senses can the idea of cause refer to the production of the whole. In the first sense the whole would be a mere consequence, like mathematical deduction, and, in the second sense, the whole would be like a human work, which would imply anthropomorphism. We must not, then, say "that there is a genesis of the whole, but rather that the whole is a genesis."[2] Such, in essence, is Le Roy's argument.

We shall find again later on, when we study the views of Sartre, on the subject of creation, one of the elements of this objection, and we shall have to discuss it more thoroughly. Here I shall confine myself to Le Roy's accusation that we reduce all causality to an act of free will, which, in his view, would expose us to pure anthropomorphism. (This consists in attributing to beings and to the phenomena of nature, in order to explain them, what belongs only to man.) Now, on the other hand, we meet here once again the postulate we have just been discussing in connection with Brunschvicg, and which consists in simply denying, but perhaps in a still more arbitrary way, the validity of the method of analogy—in denying that the idea of causality can apply in senses that are proportionately alike though otherwise different, and to all

[1] Ed. Le Roy, *ibid.*, p. 93.
[1] Ed. Le Roy, *ibid.*, p. 93.

the beings in the world. On the other hand, while agreeing with Le Roy that the whole is not a completed thing but a becoming, a genesis, a progressive causality, unlike our human creations of which the result is produced immediately, and once produced goes no further, it remains nevertheless for us to explain the genesis in which the whole consists, and to look for its cause and principle. There seems no reason why a thing which is a genesis should not itself have a cause, or why it should be necessarily its own cause. If we refuse to look for a cause of its becoming, as such (with which, of its very meaning, it is identical), it remains for us to look for the cause of its being or existence. Le Roy hides from himself this necessity by using the word "genesis" in two different senses: "genesis" may refer to a change or becoming of some kind, or to a coming into existence. Plainly when he identifies the two meanings Le Roy in his turn begs the whole question.

4. *Jean-Paul Sartre*. The objections brought forward by Sartre are much more radical than the previous ones, for they aim at showing that the idea of God is contradictory in itself. They may be summed up under three main headings.[1]

In his great work, *L'Etre et le Néant*, Sartre distinguishes the "in-itself", which is the being, "massive, obscure, dark, without any opening", and the "for-itself", which is the consciousness of self. Now, he says, the one excludes the other: the "in-itself", being impervious, cannot admit consciousness of itself, which supposes, in order to exist, some interplay in the being—the "for-itself" or consciousness tends to destroy the "in-itself"; in the end it will be stifled. If this is so, the idea of God, the idea of a being in which the "in-itself" and the "for-itself" are absolutely identical, is a contradictory idea and self-destructive, since it combines two incompatible elements, which exclude one another.

The answer which has to be made to this argument is that it is entirely based on the philosophy of Sartre, and on the conception of the "in-itself" and the "for-itself" and their

[1] J.-P. Sartre, *L'Etre et le Néant*, pp. 121-7, 133, 358-64.

relations. This conception, however, is very much open to criticism, for it demands that we implicitly regard the "in-itself" as like matter. If the "in-itself" (or being) is matter, plainly it excludes the "for-itself", consciousness and mind. Yet in fact the "in-itself", as such, is so far from being reducible to matter that matter, being of itself pure multiplicity and dispersal in space, is, in this respect, the absolute opposite of the "in-itself" or of being. Its being can only come to it from a unifying principle distinct from itself and of an immaterial nature, form, soul or mind, which is "for-itself" or analogous to "for-itself". From this point of view the idea of God, instead of being contradictory, as Sartre wishes to say, is in itself supremely intelligible: God is the absolute "in-itself", because he is the absolute "for-itself", that is to say "in-itself" utterly transparent to itself and wholly coincident with itself.

Again (leaving aside for the moment Sartre's objection to the idea of creation, to which we must return later, when dealing with creation) Sartre asserts that the idea of God cannot be validly presented as that of a necessary being. Indeed he says that God is without any source of being which can justify his being, and he is, therefore, *contingent*. This follows from the fact that God cannot have this source either in himself, for he would be divided, so to speak, into "in-itself" and "for-itself" (the act of being his own source implies this duality, but the one excludes the other)—nor in a possible being, higher than himself or before himself, since the possible is nothing apart from being, and he could not have anything possible previous to being.

I reply that it is true in one sense that God is "without source", since he is himself the source, not only in so far as he gives being to himself, but in so far as he *is*, purely and simply, for there is nothing, not even a logical priority, between the source and the being (they are only "two" to our thought, which is inadequate to express the absolute simplicity of the divine being). But this only means that God contains in himself the full reason for his own existence. From this point of view he excludes from himself all contingency, and is, in the true and absolute sense, the necessary being and the only being who is necessary.

It is clear that these are not serious difficulties against the notion of God. Nevertheless they are valuable in making us aware of what is involved in a consistent idea of God. From this point of view Sartre, in common with the other philosophers whose objections we have just been examining, helps us to advance our knowledge of God. This discussion (somewhat abstract, I am afraid, but that cannot be avoided) has already allowed us to go part of the way towards grasping the exact meaning and scope of the metaphysical proofs for God and towards clearing our path of the obstacles which block it. As a result the discussion which follows will be much plainer. However, before embarking on this, we must examine shortly a point of view which is at the opposite pole to that of the thinkers who have just been under review. It consists in saying that the existence of God is of itself so evident that it requires no proof, but is manifest once we grasp the meaning of the word God. This is what is called the ontological argument.

II. *THE METAPHYSICAL PROOFS*

A. *The* a priori *proof*

1. *The ontological argument.* The *a priori* proof, known as the ontological argument, was worked out by St Anselm (1032-1109) in his *Proslogion,* and repeated by Descartes in his *Fifth Meditation.* At first sight this argument entrances the mind by its elegance and apparent rigour, but, on reflection, involves great difficulties. It consists in proving the existence of God by starting from the simple idea of God. It can be put in the following logical form : The idea of God is that of an absolutely perfect being. But the perfect being necessarily exists, for how could it be perfect unless it existed? Therefore God necessarily exists.

This proof has been rightly attacked because it passes un-
justifiably from the logical to the ontological order. It is quite
true that, if I conceive God as the perfect being, I must also
conceive him as existing, for otherwise my thought will not
be consistent. But that is not enough to prove that God really
exists, for it can only apply to an existence in thought. The
reasoning of the ontological argument deals only with ideas,
there is no *a priori* guarantee that the idea of a perfect being
existing of itself is more than a logical fiction, corresponding
to nothing real outside the mind. This idea only acquires
validity and consistency if it is truly formed by the mind as
a consequence of the demands of real being and is grasped
through experience. It is this same criticism which Kant has
put forward under a slightly different form. The mistake in
the ontological argument, he says, lies in making existence an
attribute, in stating that "existence is a perfection". In fact
existence is not an attribute; it does not make up part of the
concept or definition of a thing: "a hundred real thalers con-
tain no more than a hundred possible thalers". Existence is
the putting in being of the attributes themselves. Consequently
we have no right to include existence in the definition of the
concept as one of its attributes.

This criticism is certainly valid, if we take St Anselm's
argument in the form I have given it. Nevertheless the argument has survived every attempt to refute it, and this makes
one think that it contains something to justify the charm it
has always exercised on the human mind, and that it includes
an element of truth which should be preserved. The argument
seems to imply a thorough understanding of the inner requirements of the idea of God, of a being in whom essence and
existence are not really distinct and are only one thing, so
much so that here, contrary to what is true of the rest of
reality, to grasp an essence is equivalent to apprehending an
existence *in its very necessity*. It is precisely this point on
which Descartes has most insisted, saying that his argument
does not start from the word "God", but from a real and

objective essence or nature, and hence always remains, from its beginning (the nature of God) to its conclusion (the existence of God), in the real order.[1] Whatever may be thought of the Cartesian view, this aspect of the ontological argument makes it clear that St Thomas, who had refuted the Anselmian proof before Kant, was far from taking up a purely negative attitude towards it. If the assertion, "God exists", he says, is not and cannot be *a priori* evidence for us, in itself, that is, from the standpoint of what God's nature demands, it is evident that God exists, since essence and existence being identical in him, he cannot not exist. He exists necessarily. It is this intrinsic evidence, this absolute bond, this identity of essence and existence, which is expressed in the ontological argument. Its mistake, as St Thomas and Kant have seen, lies undoubtedly in its attempt to prove God *a priori,* but its truth lies also in grasping that, if God exists, he exists necessarily.[2]

Thus the ontological argument can make us understand, in Blondel's words, that the idea of God is "auto-affirmative", and that the ontological proof, "defective in us, has in itself its necessary force", or, to speak more accurately, that what is "auto-affirmative" is the very essence of God, of which Descartes says that it exists by a sort of superabundance of being (*causa sui*). And without doubt it is because we have a certain notion, obscure and confused, of the essence of God (for we are "in his image and likeness") that the idea of God has in us this strange power of auto-affirmation. In this way the ontological proof is justified up to a certain point, but it is, taken in this sense, not so much a proof as a statement of what we are aware of and an explanation of it. I agree, then, with Sertillanges in saying that what is left in St Anselm's proof is "a deep awareness of God, an admirable analysis of the implications of the first cause, a powerful psychological

[1] Descartes, *Réponses aux Premières objections,* § 12.
[2] Cf. St Thomas, *De Veritate,* q. 10, art. 12, ad 2: *Contra Gentiles,* ch. X; *Summa Theol.,* Ia, Q.2, art. 1.

effort, and expression of religious feeling which fully redeems the logical weakness of the proof", and that, if there is no proof in the strict sense, "there is, in anticipation of proof, as an illustration of it, a strong and imposing systematic construction of the hypothesis of God".[1]

2. *The proof from the idea of perfection.* The Cartesian proof from the idea of perfection or of the infinite has often been linked to the ontological argument. Yet Descartes put this as an *a posteriori* proof, that is, as a passage from effect to its true and adequate cause. "Being finite", he says, "I should not have the idea of an infinite substance, if it had not been given me by a substance which was really infinite."[2] In other words, we could not possibly have the sense of our imperfection (ignorance, doubt, error, moral evil and sin) which is so profound, universal and distressing—Pascal speaks of our "wretchedness"—if we did not relate it to a perfection which we do not possess, that is, if we did not think of it in reference to perfection of which we have the notion though we cannot explain it as derived from ourselves.

Descartes always vigorously denied that he reasoned *a priori,* that is, that he started from the *idea* of perfection. On the contrary he starts from the presence in us, who are imperfect, of the idea of the perfect or the infinite. Now to explain the presence or the reality of this idea we must agree that it has been given us by a being who is really perfect and infinite and that it is innate. An imperfect being who has the idea of perfection, says Descartes, cannot be explained through himself, that is, as being the cause of himself, because, if he was the cause of himself, he would necessarily be given all the perfection of which he has the idea. Therefore he can only exist through someone else, and this other person can only be explained by someone else again, if, having the idea of the perfect, he is himself imperfect. As we cannot go to

[1] A. D. Sertillanges, *Les Grandes Thèses de la philosophie thomiste* (Paris, Bloud et Gay, 1928), p. 58.
[2] Descartes, *Third Meditation.*

infinity, we must necessarily conclude that there exists a being who is cause of himself, and possesses all the perfections of which he has the idea. It is this being that we call God.

This well-known argument calls for the same criticism as the ontological argument. We can dispute its being a proof in the strict sense, because the idea of perfection we have is not basically that of an absolutely and infinitely perfect thing, but of a perfect thing which is in some sense relative. Nevertheless we must not neglect the profound significance of the Cartesian argument; it makes us realize our imperfection and our aspiration for the absolutely true and good as involved in one another. How is this double tendency to be explained? There is really in us a certain idea or sense of a perfection and of an infinite which stirs us and moves us from within, and which cannot be explained without reference to an absolute being and good. We have seen that this is the meaning of the proof from the soul's aspirations, but there is a difference: Descartes meant to proceed by way of efficient causality (the idea of the infinite can have no other cause than God), while the argument from the aspirations for infinite happiness and goodness rests on final purpose (it is the end which is cause of all the rest: if God did not exist, the aspiration for the infinite—or idea of the infinite—would be an effect without a cause, which is absurd).

The Cartesian proof can make us understand once again that the idea of God is in a sense innate in us. The idea is not adequately formed from the beginning (nor can we ever have an adequate idea of God, for God infinitely exceeds our understanding). But it can be said to be innate potentially, in the demands of reason and of the human heart, and from this point of view, as I mentioned above, it precedes, and is at the base of, all the reasoning by which we justify and explain it. A whole tradition, which runs through the history of thought from Plato, St Augustine and St Thomas, down to Lachelier and Lavelle, is unanimous on this point, and fundamentally Descartes fully agrees.

B. *The* a posteriori *proofs*

1. *General outline of the* a posteriori *proofs*. St Thomas Aquinas, in a series of famous passages, has shown how the "hypothesis of God", which is impressed on us by all the reasons which we have just been studying, is confirmed, from different points of view, by the arguments which all go to prove the necessity of a being possessing certain uncreated attributes: unchangeable being, first cause of all, necessary being existing of itself, absolute value, all-controlling intelligence. I shall explain these different arguments, but first I shall take them together, in a synthetic form, so as to make more directly clear what is the feature common to them all. I think it will then be seen more easily that these arguments in their technical form only express the deep intuition of common sense, applied to reality, and experiencing the radical insufficiency of reality to explain itself.

We start from the simplest and least disputable experience. All we know around us in nature appears to us as a chain of existences that follow one another and modify one another, forming a number of rings firmly joined together. We recognize, in the realities given to our experience, a succession of qualities or attributes which communicate with one another and are exchanged among the different beings—values which are arranged in varying degrees—results, sometimes partial, sometimes general, which become gradually more general, and together form a universe. "It is", writes Sertillanges, "an order of inter-connecting series, a cosmos with wide subdivisions, but in which the whole is joined together. One thing comes from another, which itself draws its value from another, and that from yet another. An effect comes from a cause, and this, in order to act, requires another cause, which requires again another." In the order of things which makes the universe a totality, "an element attaches itself to a group, this becomes an element in another group, large groups are formed".[1] To use a word familiar to philosophers all this shows a great "conditioning", through which, on different levels, in different respects, under different forms, in various degrees, being and the benefits of being move round, that is to say, order and unity, goodness and beauty.

Now how are we to explain this chain of events? What is implied by the fact of its existence and of its regular action? I showed above that the objections drawn from Kant's criticism of the principle of causality, or based on emphasizing the continuity of the universe, considered as a whole, either do not affect the issue, or cannot get rid of the problem of the cause of the universe, and of what Hamelin called "its terribly vast and profound organization".[2] We have to recognize that the world shows itself to us as a vast chain of events of many kinds, and that we are obliged to inquire into its meaning.

The principle which forms the key to the discussion is that, in any order of things, nothing gives what it does not possess. That which it has, either it has from itself, in virtue of its own essence or nature, or else it receives it from something else, which in its turn either receives it from something else, or else has it of itself. The very movement of exchange, the moving round of being, shows that there are sources, and, beyond all intermediate things, however many these may be or may be supposed to be, original sources, first being, first perfections, ultimate reasons of all that appears. The demands of reason take us further, and make us realize that these various sources must depend on a single source which is absolutely first. Unless, indeed, we come back to a principle which is absolutely first, nothing is explained, since, in the order of causes, it is the first which produces them all, the others being only intermediate and only able to transmit movement or being. A canal is no explanation of the water

[1] A.-D. Sertillanges, *Les Grandes Thèses de la philosophie thomiste*, p. 59.

[2] O. Hamelin, *Essai sur les éléments principaux de la représentation* (Paris, 1907), p. 458.

which passes through it; only its source can explain the river.

We can, therefore, understand that in a causal series it is impossible to go back to an unlimited extent, and hence that we must necessarily come to an absolutely first cause. The term "first" is itself, as we shall see better later on, quite inadequate, since the source or absolute principle is, of its very meaning, transcendent to all the series of causes and effects, which depend upon it; it does not make up one of a number with them, and hence is only "first" in our hopelessly imperfect way of speaking. In any case it is clear that neither the length of the canal nor the number of intermediate things can ever relieve us of the need to find the principle and the source. Even if the canal were indefinitely long, and the number of intermediate terms infinite, this makes no difference. On the contrary, if you suppose there is no first source, the intermediate things will have nothing to transmit. The canals will remain empty and will provide nothing, precisely because of themselves they have nothing.[1]

In order, however, to grasp fully the form of this argument, we must avoid a mistake which is often made (Kant bases on this very mistake his criticism of the argument from contingency), between merely coordinate causes and subordinate causes. Merely coordinate causes only refer to pure succession and not to the existence of the thing conditioned. These causes might be infinite in number, so that in going through them you would never reach the first term. From this point of view

---

[1] It is scarcely necessary to point out that the *first source* of movement cannot be matter, in spite of the view held by philosophers of antiquity (Pre-socratics), of the Middle Ages (e.g. David de Dinant: cf. Ch. III, 3), and of modern times, such as Marx and Engels, to whom "movement is the mode of existence of matter, the manner of being of matter" (Fr. Engels, *L'Anti-Düring*, ed. Costes, 1931, vol. 1, pp. 74–5). For matter can never be a *first* cause, in the sense just explained, but only a *physical* and *univocal* cause, itself subordinate and moved, because on any hypothesis it is an element of the whole which is in movement. That is what I have already argued when discussing an objection of Le Roy (see above p. 39 and below pp. 56–8).

we can agree with St Thomas that there is no intrinsic contradiction in the concept of an "eternal world", or, more
exactly (since God alone is eternal), in that of a world which
has always existed, without any beginning in time. The argument of the hen and the egg, so often quoted in a popular
form, is here quite ineffective, for there is no reason for
stopping in the regression as we go on from egg to hen and
hen to egg. In this order of things, we can go on to infinity.
So too the succession of generations which bring living beings
into existence can very well be unlimited, no limit being
assignable in the series. (We know that this is not so, but it is
Revelation which tells us, natural science itself being unable
to say anything absolutely certain about it.) This is because
successive generations only transmit life; they are sufficient
to explain this transmission, if that is required. What, however, they cannot explain is life itself and existence, that is,
life and actual existence, at every moment of a duration
(which can be thought of as infinite). The reason is that, as
Descartes well puts it, "we are concerned less with the cause
which produced me in the past than with that which con-
serves me [that is, which makes me exist] at the present
moment".[1] Thus we realize that we shall never reach God by
seeking a beginning in time for the universe, and that a true
demonstration of God's existence must not be based on the
fact that the universe began because this beginning is in no
way demanded by the nature of things, and the demonstration, postulating a beginning in time, would also postulate
God, and there would be a vicious circle.

Kant's mistake in what he calls "the first antinomy of pure
reason" is not, as has often been asserted, that he held reason
could prove both that the world had a beginning and that it
did not have one. For, as we have just seen, reason (if it leaves
aside Revelation) can prove both. His mistake is that he did
not understand that these two demonstrations are not really
contradictory, since they do not look at the question from the

[1] Descartes, *Third Meditation*.

same point of view. The first is based on the impossibility of ever stopping in the regression from effect to cause and from cause to effect (the causes are regarded as simply coordinates in the transmission of causality). The second is based on the impossibility of going on to infinity in the order of the absolute reason for beings and their properties and for being in general. The whole question lies there. A man has a son; he himself had a father, and his father had a father. There is no reason to stop in this regression, which might (theoretically) be "eternal". But on the other hand, we must stop if we consider the causes which *actually* depend on one another for the production of their causality. These causes cannot be infinite in number because, unless there is an absolutely first cause communicating the causal power, existence and life, nothing will be produced, no generation or causality will be possible.

Take some fact, for instance, a particular man who actually exists. We ask, not the cause by which he came into existence, but the cause by which he exists at *the present moment*. The cause sufficient to account for this is plainly not his father, who only transmits life, but the sun and the heat which it communicates, for the exercise of his vital activities. Without this heat life will be impossible and will cease at once. Now the sun itself depends on other cosmic causes without which it will produce nothing, and will not exist as a source of heat. Without these cosmic causes the heat of the sun will not exist, and life will no longer be possible. We can, if we like, think of these cosmic causes on which the heat of the sun depends as themselves depending on other causes, from which they derive their efficacy and reality. But in any case, however far back we wish to press our search for a source of causality, we must only stop at a true source, the first principle of those activities which, one after another, explain here and now and at every moment the actual existence and activities of this man and of all things. Otherwise there would be nothing, neither beings nor activities. The working of a machine can never be explained by its wheels and the various parts of its machinery (even if they should be infinite in number). These must be set in motion by a first source of activity and energy. Without this source the machine stops, since no movement is transmitted. Now this is true of existence itself. Unless we acknowledge a first source of being and existence, as such, that is, in their absolute reality at every moment, there will be neither being nor existence. There will be nothing whatever, neither being nor becoming.

Thus we necessarily come to the ultimate origins of being and movement ("movement" here being synonymous with all the forms of energy which manifest themselves in the world), of perfection of every kind and degree, to the very source of order. These first sources exist. Reason demands them absolutely, for without them nothing will be intelligible, and it is the search for them which in the end is the business of every science. For science is wholly directed to the discovery of causes, and of the most universal causes. On the level of positive science, research seeks, it is true, only to determine the empirical connections of phenomena, and does not seek to discover the laws of succession. But the sciences have a higher and more remote aim, even within the context of these positive principles, and the immense developments of modern physical science, exemplified by such names as Einstein and Louis de Broglie, are sufficient witness of this. By bold generalizations, sweeping hypotheses, they aim at unifying, if possible, under a single law, the whole mass of particular laws, and at reaching the very first principle (of course physical) of the whole universe. This attempt has already produced wonderful results. Nevertheless, even granting it reaches its end and is crowned with complete success, we must not suppose that then all research will necessarily be finished, and that the demands of reason will be finally satisfied. The question will then inevitably arise whether these first principles, or, if you like, the single first principle of the physical universe, should be regarded as absolutely first, that is, whether, as I said above, we should then be dealing with ultimate sources or origins, or only canals. However big the canal, even though it were the only canal, nothing can prevent it being a canal and a means for carrying water, an intermediary. The first principle must necessarily suffice for itself; it must justify itself by itself, by its own nature, and show itself as necessary, that is, show itself such that we can conceive it, in virtue of the demands of universal being, as dependent neither for existence nor for its activities on anything other than itself.

This is what we call the necessary being, not merely in the sense that in fact it must not perish or change, but in the sense that to perish or to change is utterly impossible for it on account of its very nature. This amounts to saying that the necessary being contains in itself its whole reason, so that it can receive nothing, either as being or as intelligible, but, on the contrary, that everything else receives from it intelligibility and being.

I have outlined the most general aim and form of this inquiry. All that I shall have to say about the different metaphysical arguments which prove the existence of God or, if you like, which prove the inescapable need and absolute validity of the hypothesis of God, will merely apply the principle I have just explained. I have only to repeat the principle, looking at it from different possible aspects, and showing how it leads us to accept the existence of God, as pure act, first cause, the necessary being, subsistent perfection and supreme intelligence. It is not a matter, however, simply of repeating what has just been said, but of bringing out precisely, in each case, the application of the argument, and of replying to difficulties which this may suggest.

2. *Pure act.* The argument, which leads us to assert the absolute reality of that which Aristotle and all later philosophers have called pure act, is the argument drawn from the movement, that is the "becoming", of things and of the world. St Thomas, who considers this the simplest and clearest

argument of all, explains it as follows. "It is plain, as our senses tell us, that some things move in this world. But everything that moves is moved by something else. It is impossible that, from the same point of view, a thing should at the same time be mover and moved, this is, that it should by itself give itself movement. Thus, if a thing moves, it must be moved by something else. If that by which it is moved, itself moves, this too must be moved by something else, and this again by something else. But we cannot go on to infinity, for then there would be no first mover, and consequently there would be no other mover, because secondary movers are only movers because moved by the first mover, just as the stick only moves because moved by the hand. Therefore we must come to a first mover, moved by nothing else, and this first mover is God."[1]

This argument calls for two remarks. First, it is not a question of supposing that particular things and the world were set first in a state of immobility, without any internal "becoming", for on such an hypothesis the communication of movement obviously demands God: this would be to beg the question. We can and must agree that things are necessarily and essentially in movement, and subject, by their very nature, to a permanent process of becoming. But this does not by any means dispense us from seeking the first cause of the becoming and the movement. Even though things may move in virtue of their nature, this is not, and cannot be, due to themselves or in virtue of themselves. Their becoming and their movement necessarily and actually, at every instant of their duration, require a first principle which gives them their movement. Otherwise there could be no movement or becoming. Whether essential or accidental to things the movement demands a first cause, and one which does not move. I may add that the term "movement" does not only refer to local movement, but refers in general to any change from one manner of being to another. Thus human understanding is

[1] St Thomas, *Summa Theol.*, I, Q.2, art. 3.

itself a movement, from the very fact that it is only exercised by "discourse", that is, as the word implies, by going from one idea to another.

Again, it would be quite wrong to think that the argument leads us, by speaking of pure act, to assert the existence of a "supreme immobility", as Le Roy says, that is, of a reality without any activity. If we call the first cause, or pure act, "motionless" ("immutable" would be a better term), it is only in the sense that its activity does not result from an ever fresh increase of being and perfection. For such activity would imply a radical lack, and therefore would necessarily mean that it was subject to a superior energy, since nothing can give itself what it does not possess. In other words the idea of "immobility" (or immutability) only implies in the universal first mover a fullness of being which excludes all privation. That is why St Thomas declares elsewhere[2] that the proof from movement can take us to a first mover who moves himself (that is, to a being who has in himself the absolute reason of his activity) quite as well as to a first mover who cannot move. Thus, adds St Thomas, "Plato and Aristotle are basically in agreement; they only differ in the mode of expression".

3. *The first cause of all.* The preceding argument has shown us that the first principle, unmoved in the sense of immutable, is also active, as being cause of the movement and becoming of the world, but with an activity which, being derived entirely from itself, involves no passivity at all in it (while the things in the world, being movers which are moved, are passive to their own activity). That is why it is called pure act. The second argument goes on to prove the universal efficient causality of the first mover. But we should notice that, so far as movement or becoming moved are concerned, the divine causality was shown in the first argument. Here we have to consider efficient causality, or the causality of things in rela-

[1] Cf. Ed. Le Roy, *Le Problème de Dieu*, p. 22.
[1] St Thomas, *Commentary on the Physics of Aristotle*, VII, 1.

tion to one another. That is the present question, and we have to ask if efficient causality can be explained without God. We shall see that the third argument, which starts from the contingent character of the world, also leads us to see an aspect of God's universal causality, that which is concerned with the very being of the world.

I shall quote once again the words of St Thomas in their original form, on account of their great clarity. "We find", he says, "in the sensible world efficient causes (the efficient cause is, in general, that by which anything exists, or becomes something). Now it is impossible that a thing should be its own efficient cause, for, if it was, this thing would exist before it existed, which is absurd. But we cannot go to infinity in the series of efficient causes, for in the whole series of causes, the first is cause of that which is intermediate, and this is cause of the last (whether there are many intermediate causes or not). If the cause is removed, the effect is also removed. Hence, if there is no first cause, there will be no last cause, and no intermediate cause. But to proceed to infinity in the series of efficient causes amounts to saying there is no first cause; if there is no first cause, neither is there any effect, nor intermediate causes. This is manifestly false, as experience shows. We must, then, agree there is a first cause; which all call God."[1]

It can be seen that here again the general theme recurs which I explained at the beginning. When drawn out it consists in saying that it is impossible to go to infinity in the order of causes which are subordinate to one another. I need not return to this subject, but need only conclude the discussion by mentioning two very important points. First we should notice (as I have already shown above, in passing) that the universal cause cannot be a first member in the series of causes: it must in the established phrase transcend, that is, be utterly outside, the whole series and all the causal series. For, if it was only the first link in a chain, or the first member

[1] St Thomas, *Summa Theol.*, I, Q. 2, art. 3.

in a series (however far back it is conceived), it would of its very meaning be a part of the series considered in its totality. It might then undoubtedly transmit gradually the causal power to other elements of the series, but could not be the absolute source.

Here I may mention an example already suggested, that of a machine made up of a multitude of wheels connected together and transmitting from one to another an initial energy (or efficient causality). I claim that the source of the energy cannot reside in the first wheel, and that on the contrary it must be found outside the machine, precisely because the first wheel, which as such is part of the machine, cannot of itself produce efficient causality. This will only result from the intervention (whether direct or indirect makes no difference) of man. Now all this applies in due proportion to the first cause. If we wish to consider the first cause as the first member in the series of causes, we must necessarily take it as being of the same nature as the other members, and hence as a cause which is itself caused (that is, as the effect of another cause) and as receiving from outside itself the causal power or energy which it transmits. We should then have to explain why and how this first cause began to be a cause. In virtue of the principle that nothing is its own cause we should have to go back to a further and higher cause, which would itself have to be regarded as first, but this is contradictory. Hence it follows that the absolutely first cause must necessarily transcend all the causal series and of itself be the cause, the uncaused and the uncreated cause. Thus we have established a point of first importance, to which we shall have to return, a point which concerns the absolute transcendence of God. God, if he exists, is not only higher than the world, but he is utterly independent of it, both in his being and in his activity. Every conception of God which regards him from whatever standpoint or in whatever degree, as dependent on the world, will be radically contradictory in itself, for it will be equivalent, while affirming God, to denying him.

There is, however, another objection which has been raised against the argument for proving the existence of a first cause, uncaused and transcendent to the whole universe. It is the second point which we have to examine. The objection is based on the hypothesis of causality in a circle. As we know, many teachers of antiquity accepted something of this kind under the name of an "everlasting return", and Nietzsche in our days has renewed the theory. Now this theory claims that there is no need of a first cause, because in a circle no member can be looked on as first. Even granting, however, that this hypothesis is sound, it does not affect the argument, and what I said about the metaphysical proofs in general has already given the answer plainly. For the fact that causality is linear, or that it is circular, only affects its transmission and not its origin in the absolute sense. This origin cannot be found within the universe, because, as stated in the hypothesis itself, it cannot be found in any of the members which compose it, since they are all, one after another, effects and causes, causes and effects. It might be said, no doubt, that the first principle is the universe itself, considered as a single whole. But this again cannot be taken as a solution. For the whole, as such and of its very meaning, would not exist apart from the members of which it is composed. It results from their order and harmonious working, but it must itself be explained as a whole or as a unity, for a whole must have a cause of its unity. Further, while admitting that the whole is, as such, a causality which, though immensely complex, can be reduced to the cyclic unity supposed by the hypothesis, this causality, this total efficient causality, must, as our argument shows, exist either of itself or from another. Since it cannot exist of itself, because the whole, far from being transcendent to the members, is nothing else than their sum, its existence must come from outside itself, that is (since we cannot go to infinity in this order of things) from God. Thus the hypothesis we are considering would give no explanation at all of the whole as existing as a being. This last point brings me to the third argument.

4. *The necessary being.* This new argument runs parallel to the last. It is based on the fact of the contingency of the world, and shows that this contingent world demands absolutely, for its explanation, a necessary being. That is to say, the very nature of a being which is finite and in a state of becoming, requires a cause of its being, which is itself the necessary being, such, that is, as to exist of itself. Hence this proof does not appeal to the hypothesis of a causal hierarchy within the world. It starts simply from the being of the existing world, and shows that its very contingency, which is intrinsic to the being of the world, demands absolutely a necessary being, necessary of its very nature and essence.

The argument runs as follows. We show that the world is composed of a multitude of beings, which are born, change and perish, that these are made up of elements and have been formed from these elements, and as such are by their very nature subject to decomposition. (Science tells us that these beings are subject to continuous processes of dissolution.) Now beings so formed cannot have in themselves the adequate reason for their existence; that is, they are contingent. A being which has in itself and of itself the adequate reason for its existence must exist always and necessarily. It cannot not be; it can neither begin nor perish, since manifestly a being which begins and ceases has not in itself any necessity for its being. Nor can it be subject to change since, as we have seen in the first argument, change or becoming requires an unmoved mover, that is, a cause of change which is itself unmovable or immutable. It follows that beings who come into existence and who perish and, in general, beings subject to becoming, must necessarily have the absolute reason of their existence in something else. Since, however, we cannot go to infinity in the search for the first cause of being, we must conclude that the universe, so far as it is formed of contingent beings, can only be explained, as regards its being

or existence, by a necessary being existing of itself, in virtue
of its own nature, by which everything that is exists.[1]

As with the preceding arguments, a few remarks are needed
to make clear the meaning of the proof and to reply to objections. It should be noticed first of all that the argument does
not, as is sometimes alleged against it, involve a vicious circle.
The objection is this: by the very fact that you speak of contingent beings (that is, beings who do not have the reason of
their existence in themselves) you imply there is the necessary
being. It is not a proof, but a sheer begging of the question.
As a matter of fact, however, as we have seen, the term
"contingency" only expresses primarily an experience or a fact
which is plain and quite undeniable, namely, that of the
universal process of generation and corruption, to which all
things in the world are subject. It is true that in this very
experience and in the abstract term which expresses it (contingency), the existence of the necessary being is contained.
But it is only contained virtually, just as the consequence is
contained in the antecedent. Actual knowledge of this existence is by no means presupposed, but has to be proved (as
we have just seen, by the fact that beings subject to becoming
are absolutely incapable of explaining of themselves their
own existence). This confirms a remark I made before: the
proof for God has an intuitive character, in the sense that the
existence of God is grasped by a single look at facts or principles which support it. Of course as such it involves a process of reasoning, but this can only be made explicit
afterwards (sometimes with difficulty), without the intuition
losing anything of its value and richness.

The objection has also been made to the argument that
even though the individuals taken separately are contingent,
as a group or as a sum they can exist of themselves. I reply
that if any of the members taken apart has no reason for
existence in itself, however much you put together these contingent beings, you will never make a necessary being. But

[1] St Thomas, *Summa Theol.*, I, Q. 2, art. 3.

could it be said that to the sum of the contingent beings there could be added a synthetic principle, which could confer unity and itself be necessary? But, first, this could not be a reason in the strict sense for the being or existence of events as such, but only a reason for their becoming and their coherence. Again, this principle which would make the world a single whole, could not without contradiction be itself considered as a being which is necessary of itself, because the hypothesis implies that it is itself involved in the becoming of the world, or, more precisely, that it is identified with this becoming, because it is the first member of the whole. I said above, when explaining the argument for the universal cause, that this cause must transcend all the causal series. The absolutely necessary being is thus absolutely transcendent and cannot possibly be, from any standpoint or in any degree, a member in the world.

Consequently we must admit that there exists an absolutely necessary being, and we must also admit as part of the same argument that this necessary being, which has in itself the full reason for its being, absolutely transcends the world, and is that which we call God or the perfect being. For the fact of having in itself the full reason of its being and self-existence implies of its very meaning *perfect identity of essence* and existence. These are two expressions with exactly the same meaning. Now here we have a property of the perfect being, since the being which exists of its own essence is such that nothing in it limits it or confines the unlimited fullness of its being or existence. Thus the necessary being is the perfect being. It is also the infinite: this term is true of it in the sense of fullness of being, but not in the negative sense that it is undetermined, incomplete and potential. This would be contradictory in reference to the divine infinity, which is, as we have seen, pure act. Again, the perfect and infinite is necessarily above the material and corporal order, which is by nature limited, finite, multiple and potential. The perfect is, thus, mind.

Kant has tried to show that this reasoning is nothing but the ontological argument, which he considers a sophism, as I pointed out above. He thinks we can only assert that the necessary is the perfect in virtue of the implicit argument that "perfect being is necessary, that is, necessarily exists", which is the very formula of the ontological argument. This criticism, however, of Kant must be rejected. We began, as has been explained, by establishing *a posteriori*, that is, starting from the world, the existence of the necessary being, and drew the conclusion that reflection makes us realize that this necessary being is God (that which is perfect and infinite). Now this has no connection with the ontological argument, which, in the form refuted by Kant, consists in joining together two concepts in the abstract and independently of experience. Here, on the contrary, we have recognized in an existing thing (necessary being) the perfections which it necessarily possesses. Thus we keep entirely in the real order, in the order of being.

5. *Subsistent perfection*. We see how, in virtue of the demands made upon the intelligence by the realities which we grasp in experience, we gradually reach, not only the existence of God, but also some knowledge of his nature. The argument from the degrees of being helps by another way to confirm the certitude at which we have arrived that the necessary being is also the perfect or infinite being, that is, God.

Let us start from the standpoint of beauty (a degree of being or of perfection) manifested by things in various ways. We argue: if beauty is found in many things, it must be produced in them by a single cause, which is absolute beauty. This quality, common to many things of different kinds, cannot belong to these things by reason of their own nature. If it could, we should not be able to explain how beauty is found in them in different degrees. For if they were this beauty of their very essence, they would necessarily possess it in perfection, without any limit or restriction. The argument applies on similar grounds to all perfections or qualities which can be raised so as to apply to the absolute: being, unity, truth, goodness, intelligence and will. So true is this that we have to say that the first principle must necessarily be perfect being, absolute unity, infinite truth, goodness, beauty, reason and will.

Descartes, as we have seen, made use of an argument of this kind in his proof of God through the idea of the perfect and infinite. He said: A being which is imperfect (because it doubts and is often mistaken), but which possesses the idea of perfection, cannot have this idea by reason of its own nature, for then it would give itself all the perfection of which it has the idea. Descartes concluded from this that the idea of perfection has been given to man by a being who, having by its nature the idea of perfection, must be in itself absolutely perfect. Here I am reasoning in a somewhat different way, but in a way which is close to that of Descartes. For the essential point of my argument is that the fact that there are different degrees of beauty implies that the different beings, in which these degrees are found, simply participate in a beauty which is outside of and beyond the hierarchy of limited and finite beauties, and which is, of itself and absolutely, supreme beauty, absolute beauty.

I have just attempted to harmonize the present argument with that of Descartes, and am led on to answer a difficulty which has been raised against both lines of reasoning, and which consists in regarding them as equivalent to the ontological argument. The solution I propose is not very different at root, as we shall see, from that which I put forward in connection with Descartes. The difficulty can be expressed like this: from the very fact that we can pass, whether from an imperfect being in a real order of perfection (Descartes), or, as I have argued, from the reality in different degrees of a single perfection, to the idea of a perfect being in this order, plainly we can conclude that this perfect being necessarily exists. But, as in the ontological argument, so here only a logical or ideal connection between two concepts is established, namely, that of a limited and multiple perfection and that of a perfect being. This being so, there is no proof that the perfect being really exists.

As a matter of fact this difficulty does not tell against the present argument. For I am saying that beings which possess different, and consequently unequal, degrees of perfection, cannot have in themselves the absolute reason for this perfection. They must, therefore, have it in something else which, when we reach the end (here again we cannot go on to infinity), possesses this perfection both by its own nature and in the supreme degree, or more precisely, beyond any degree and in the mode of infinity. Thus it can be seen that we do not reason about concepts, but about real things and real beings, and, consequently, that the existence, and not merely the idea, of perfection, is strictly required as supreme cause of all perfection. The argument, then, is certainly *a posteriori* and differs essentially from the ontological argument, at least as commonly understood and as refuted by Kant. Thus we have good grounds for concluding that all perfections (or degrees of being) given in experience can only be explained by a being who possesses absolutely and essentially absolute, unlimited, perfection, and who communicates it to other beings, as participating in his own infinite perfection.

In this way again we are brought to understand that what the argument demands is not merely an ideal perfection, but a subsistent perfection, that is, such as exists in itself and of itself. For this argument, too, like the others, seeks a reason of being; it seeks a reason or cause of the different degrees of perfection or of being. Now an ultimate reason of being is not found in an idea, but only in a *being,* in this case in a being who is cause of the perfection and possesses it essentially, while everything else possesses it only by participation.

These remarks lead me to describe shortly a celebrated argument connected with the preceding one, which St Augustine in particular has drawn out at length, and which was repeated in the seventeenth century by the Cartesians,

Bossuet, Fénelon, Malebranche and Leibniz.[1] Kant, too, in his work on "the only possible argument for the existence of God", suggested this argument from the eternal truths as a proof which in his eyes decisively showed the existence of God. The starting point of the argument is found in the fact that there are *eternal truths* (indeed that all truth as such is eternal), that is, truths withdrawn from all the changes of space and time. This fact, says St Augustine, is for us supremely evident, far more so than the existence of the sensible things. For we realize and see that truth is independent of our finite and passing minds. On the one hand the essences of things are unchangeably true, since of themselves they abstract from space and time (man, as existing, has begun to be, but his essence or idea—that of a sensible and rational being—is outside time). On the other hand every genuine judgement, that is, every one which claims to establish a truth, implies a reference to standards or rules which are absolutely universal, independent of the judging and reasoning mind, and valid for all minds and all times. If this is so, we have to ask where are these truths, and these absolute, eternal, standards of truth. Obviously they are not contained in any place, because they are incorporeal. Hence they can only be contained in a mind. But this mind cannot be mine, nor can it be any finite, passing, mind, since this would clearly be incapable of forming a ground for their eternity. Therefore this mind can only be an infinite mind, unchangeable and eternal, like the truths themselves which are imposed on our intelligence. It is not enough to speak here, as for example did Taine, of an "eternal axiom". An abstract truth or an ideal law cannot be the ground of the real truths of the world and of minds. The abstract is the ground for nothing, since it is nothing apart from mind. Consequently we must

---

[1] Cf. St Augustine, *Soliloquia*, I, 15, 29; *de vera religione*, 30–32; Bossuet, *De la connaissance de Dieu et de soi-même*, ch. IV; Fénelon, *Traité de l'existence de Dieu*, 2e p., ch. IV; Malebranche, *Méditations chrétiennes*, IVe Méd.; Leibniz, *Nouveaux Essais*, IV, c. 11.

necessarily come to a subsistent truth or an infinite mind, the
absolute and fundamental source of all truth. This subsistent
truth, this infinite mind, is God.

This argument from the eternal truths has been put forward
in our days by many philosophers, in particular Lachelier,
Lagneau and Lavelle. The last of these puts the proof as a
doctrine of participation, the essential idea of which is that
our finite, passing, being, by all the absoluteness that it contains and requires, both in the order of being and in that of
knowing, gradually, in the very act by which it approaches
little by little the spiritual and the inward, comes to experience a presence in which it participates, and which is that of
pure act, the absolute principle of all being and all truths.
But it is Lachelier and Lagneau who have most insisted on
the argument from the eternal truths. I quote here, to complete the account I am giving, some particularly impressive
passages from these great minds. "There is in us", says
Lachelier, "something which is not an object of [sensible]
experience and which, though closely united to our nature,
yet is no part of it. I refer to thought, which is the subject of
experience, and which establishes, and in a sense creates by
affirming it, the existence of the nature. Can we, then, represent that which is beyond our thought in the image of our
thought? Yes and no. Yes, in the sense that it is distinct from
nature, and puts itself before nature. No, in the sense that it
is not, at least for us and in actual fact, a complete being, but
a simple form, of which nature furnishes the content, and
which has not, of itself and outside of itself, life or reality.
But there is one thing which we can at least admit, though
we cannot understand it: the existence of a thought which
would have no need, as ours has, of an empirical content, but
would give itself to itself, or rather, which would be for itself
alone what ours can only be when in union with nature—a
complete being, real and living. Further, we can conceive the
existence of a double relation between this being and nature.
We can agree that it establishes nature, not as we ourselves

establish it, by a purely ideal activity which is only the recognition of a reality already given, but in a fundamental way, by an affirmation which affects and produces reality, by a *fiat*, as it may be called, which is a fact."[1] We are led the more certainly to affirm the real existence of this subsistent thought because the very truth at which we arrive, and which exceeds our finite minds, obliges us to admit that there is in us "before all experience an idea of that which ought to exist, an ideal *esse*, as Plato supposed, which ought to be the type and measure for us of the real *esse*", that is to say, of all which we assert as true about the being given in our experience.[2]

We come to Lagneau. He appeals to the argument from the eternal truths under two aspects, which are distinct and yet are bound up with one another, and which recall both St Augustine and Lachelier. Lagneau writes:

We desire to be happy, but the desire for happiness is only one form of the desire for perfection in every order. Whether in the sphere of knowledge, or of beauty, or of virtue, we desire perfection. The affirmation most natural to the heart of man is that of perfection of every kind. Knowledge or science would not exist unless, from the beginning, the end to which it tends (its perfection) was presented as real and attainable if pursued. In the same way, what meaning can there be to judgements about the intrinsic value of things, unless we believe these things can be perfect in themselves apart from any further purpose, that is, unless there is a natural perfection in things in so far as they strike our senses and mind, and which is independent of the use which can be made of them? The sensible perfection is that of beauty. We are not confined to conceiving this beauty in things as capable of indefinite increase. We conceive this as possible only because there exists already a measure for judging the gradual growth in perfection. Imperfect beauty only appears conceivable to us in relation to an absolute beauty of which it is but an incomplete

[1] J. Lachelier, "Séance de la Société de Philosophie de 19 novembre 1908", *Oeuvres*, t. II, p. 160–1.

[2] J. Lachelier, "Psychologie et Métaphysique", in *Le Fondement de l'induction*, p. 157.

manifestation. . . . To speak of the beauty of things is to grasp an absolute aspect of reality. There is, I say, an absolute of beauty. Undoubtedly it cannot be expressed, like truth properly so-called, by abstract reasoning. But it is certain that there is a true beauty. In other words, every affirmation of the beauty of a thing implies the affirmation of the absolute beauty of this form of thought by which we affirm things as beautiful; we affirm an absolute of beauty.

Now, adds Lagneau, this absolute of beauty is a reality, and "this reality is nothing else than that which belongs to God himself; this reality is God. It is not simply . . . to postulate, to lay down by a free act the existence of God, when we acknowledge some thought as true; it is to participate in the very act of God, or better, to make room for God in ourselves. . . . The world, according to Descartes, can only exist by a creative act of God which is constantly renewed. But it is not only the world which cannot exist except in that way; it is thought itself."[1] Thus Lagneau rediscovers and renews one of the essential themes of Augustinian teaching.

6. *Supreme intelligence*. The argument which takes its name from *final causes* is the best known and most popular of all. The principle on which it rests, called "the principle of finality" (in virtue of which "every agent acts for an end"), leads us to assert that the complex work of organization to reach an end (or a result) demands an intelligence to control it. This assertion can be proved as follows. A material thing does not know for what end its action or its efficient causality is framed. Still more clearly it does not know what combination of means can be capable of making it realize this end or result. The intelligence, unlike a material thing, knows the end to which it tends, and it also knows what means to employ in order to realize this end. It is intelligence which explains by its very existence the unity of beings and being itself, since unity is a necessary aspect of being. Intelligence

[1] J. Lagneau, *Célèbres leçons et fragments* (Paris, Presses Universitaires, 1950), pp. 224–5, 261–2.

alone can account for the organization of means towards an end, and consequently of the synthesis of elements, of the unifying of what is distinct, of the coordination of many things.

Thus we can see the form which the argument will take. If there is order in the world, that is, if there are beings of which the many different elements are subject to a law of unity within them which the elements cannot impose on themselves, and if the world itself, taken as a whole, is subject to an immanent order (that is, an order resulting from the harmony of its elements), it necessarily follows that a controlling intelligence is behind the universe.

Two objections can be made to this argument, first, that the unity of the universe is not evident; and, secondly, that there is a radical disorder in the world, namely, physical and moral evil. I shall not delay over this second point, because the problem of evil does not seem to raise an insuperable difficulty *here*. It is not so much a question of knowing if the order of the world is absolutely perfect, as of knowing if there is an order (an imperfect order is still an order, since imperfection can only be concerned in relation to perfection). It can be shown, moreover, that many partial "disorders" are necessary for the total order, and that they are only disorders when too restricted a view of the universe is considered. Disorder, says Bergson, is rather an order we were not expecting. An earthquake or a hailstorm are the result of physical laws, and from this point of view, show order.

The main difficulty arises from a denial of the unity of the universe. It can be summed up in this way. We cannot really succeed in finding any connection between the world of geometry and mechanics and the world of moral values. The earthquake or hailstorm which manifest a cosmic order are often a moral disorder owing to the disasters they cause. To take a more general view, we look in vain for a means to bring together thought and mechanism in the intermediate order, that is, in the order of life. Life contradicts mechanism, and cannot be identified with thought, nor thought with life. Thus the insurmountable division we see in the different aspects of the universe prevents us from admitting the internal unity of this universe, and hence the unity of the principle which is alleged to preside over our destinies. We are forced towards a kind of pluralism made up of the different orders of nature, life and morality, in which the laws of life and of morality transcend and contradict, at least to some extent, the laws of the physical order. This is the view that William James defends when he argues for a kind of polytheism, or for a variety of principles which cannot be reconciled in the universe (or, more precisely, in the universe of our experience).

We should notice that, if this were true, if, as James holds, there were a radical pluralism, we should find ourselves in the domain of the irrational, but our reason protests against such a view, for the rational is a unity. We should have to say that the absolute law which governs things does not coincide with the law of our thought, that, though what is absurd appears impossible, yet it can form the basis for things. In our own time Sartre has not hesitated to defend this theory. Nevertheless, if we look at it carefully, it involves a difficulty which is, I think, insurmountable. We see that the principles of reason are only the principles of being, in the sense that the mind formulates them through the contact of experience, not as subjective laws but as objective laws, immanent in real being. These arguments, however, will appear too abstract, and will have little power to convince anyone unless he has a gift for mathematics.

I will put it, then, in a more direct way. The separation which exists between the different orders of reality, from that of mechanism to that of psychology, and from this to that of reason and morality, does not appear to be absolute. To speak more accurately, it covers a hierarchy, and thus a certain unity: matter is at the service of life, and life at the service of morality. Mechanism is not really opposed to life

or morality, since it becomes their instrument. In other words
nature does not contradict morality; it is the field over which
morality is deployed. Lavelle in particular at the present day
has insisted on this. Undoubtedly man is more than nature
(the ancients said that he is "an addition to nature"), but he
realizes it and perfects it by using it for his spiritual ends.
In man, who is between the purely spiritual order and the
purely material order, partaking of both—of nature and mind,
mechanism and morality, determinism and freedom—the
unity of the universe is affirmed. Hence experience itself leads
us to conceive that the many reduces itself to the one: like
pure reason, it excludes pluralism. Nevertheless, however
true this may be, there is a problem of evil, and this problem
is a mystery for pure reason. I must leave its examination
for the moment. What may be said now is that evil and pain
do not absolutely break the general harmony of the universe,
since man is able to correct them in large measure, and
especially because the protest which is continuously raised by
all against evil, both physical and moral, shows that man is
utterly convinced of the reality of a more perfect order, which
gives its true meaning to the universe. Hence there is a "plan"
for the universe, and this plan, in virtue of which all the
elements of the cosmos, some of necessity, others freely, are
made to play a definite part, to form a whole, implies a controlling intelligence. That is what is meant by the argument
from final causes.

Yet it must be admitted that this argument, taken by itself,
leaves room for hesitation. The world is not infinite, and, if
a controlling intelligence is required to explain its internal
unity, strictly speaking an intelligence would suffice which
was not absolutely infinite though, of course, immensely
powerful, a demiurge who might not be God. Yet we can
also see that, on this theory, a finite intelligence, a demiurge,
and still more a cosmic form of unknown nature, not being
ultimate and being incapable of this, would need beyond
them, as the preceding proofs have shown, a being on which

they would depend. This would explain them in their turn, and would be (since in this case too we cannot go to infinity) absolutely ultimate, pure act, the perfect being. Moreover, a principle would be required which is essentially mind or thought, for, if it is true that the greater cannot come from the less, the order of mechanism, the whole system of efficient causes, connected together in a universe which is one, presents itself to us in a celebrated phrase as an "unconscious thought", and requires for its explanation a thought which creates it by thinking of it and which includes all being—to use the wonderful expression of Aristotle, "thought of thought".

Here again I must mention two kinds of difficulty which have often been raised against the argument from finality. First, an attempt has been made to find in chance an explanation of the universe. But we can see at once that to speak of chance is simply to admit our ignorance. When I turn a wheel in a lottery and win, I say "it is chance", because I cannot calculate all the causes which have contributed to the result. But these series of causes are themselves determined and the "chance" is only the result of their meeting. Thus chance, far from being the basis of order, presupposes it. Moreover, the events which we attribute to chance, in other circumstances are precisely those in which we find fickleness and lack of regularity, while order, on the contrary, is marked by regularity and stability.

It is worth while illustrating these remarks by the well-known example of the "typewriting monkeys". To make this understood I must first give some rather abstract explanations. Among the different kinds of chance there are often included instances which belong to the calculus of probabilities. To the mathematician, as we know, the probability of an event is the relation of the number of instances favourable to its production to the number of possible instances, all the instances being supposed equally possible, that is, such that no one of them has any special reason to occur and that all are completely fortuitous. Now it is from the mathematical notion of chance that the theory has been proposed of a universe started by sheer chance. It is this theory which the mathematician, E. Borel, illustrated not long ago by the example which has become famous of the "miracle of the typewriting monkeys". It is *mathematically* possible, said Borel, that the monkeys should succeed in reproducing the *Iliad*, and then all the books in all the libraries of the world, by haphazard use of a typewriter. Obviously, the probability of such a result is immeasurably small, but it is a possibility. If we suppose that the monkeys have infinite time in which to write, not only could the "miracle" be produced, but, more than that, it would be necessarily produced, because the possible combinations of signs and letters, though so many as to make the brain reel, yet are finite in number. Thus the universe could be explained : bodies can be formed by chance, starting from an original chaos, simply as a result of a movement of its elements continually renewed, which with infinite time in which to act, must, by mathematical necessity, produce, among all the possible combinations, what we call today the world.

The ancient theory of Epicurus, merely rejuvenated with the help of mathematical arguments, can be recognized here. But the theory is not strengthened, for the hypothesis of the typewriting monkeys leads to absurdity. It is truly senseless to suggest that meaning, that is, order or value, can come from the ebb and flow or movement of the elements, which, as its definition implies, contains neither meaning nor value, nor intelligence to grasp them. In order that the "miracle" of the typewriting monkeys should be plausible mathematically, first there must be, of course, monkeys and typewriters (which would at once imply an immensely complex order), but also an intelligent being, an artist, capable of giving meaning to the collection of letters and signs, called the *Iliad*. Otherwise the hypothetical monkeys, with their hypothetical typewriters, after having "composed" by chance the *Iliad*, would "compose" an indefinite number of other texts, which would have neither more nor less meaning than the *Iliad*, that is, which would be mere facts, of no particular kind whatever. This is all the more true of the universe. We speak here of a "fortunate" chance (like that of the *Iliad*). But this word "fortunate" plainly implies a judgement of value, and hence plainly postulates what the hypothesis excludes. In fact, on the supposition of the typewriting monkeys, there would be no *Iliad*, since under such circumstances this poem would be only one random arrangement, among others, of characters equally random, and without any of the value of signs (since a sign requires an intelligence), and having to reason to subsist. In the same way there would be no universe, if we suppose chance could produce a world like ours, since the structure or organization which was realized would have no more meaning and no more reason to last than any other of the structures fortuitously realized.

It would certainly need much courage to get round these difficulties. This was seen by Borel. For, when he suggested as a mathematical utopia this "miracle of the typewriting monkeys" which became so famous, he added that it would be utterly absurd to think that the world was the work of blind deities or "laws of chance". Only laws of reason could explain the fantastically complex order of the universe. To this I add, first of all, that the peculiarity of chance is to have no law or that in any case its only law is to have no law, and further that here the laws of reason, of which Borel speaks, themselves presuppose an infinite reason. Kant said in this sense: "The moral law deep in our hearts and the starry heavens above give the clearest witness there is to the existence of God". Scripture had already said in finer words: "See how the skies proclaim God's glory".

The second difficulty we have to notice will not keep us long, for the solution has already been given in this last discussion. It consists in explaining the order of the world by evolution. It is pretty clear, however, that evolution, far from being at the root of the order, presupposes it, since it works in conformity with laws, and necessary laws. Thus, evolution absolutely requires an intelligence. Efficient causes by no means exclude final causes: indeed far from it, since mechanism has no meaning or even existence except through finality. But of course there is no question of supposing that the explanation by way of finality is quite separate from the causal explanation, or is superimposed upon it. It might as well be thought that, to discover in the clock the action and intention of the clockmaker, it was necessary to establish the presence of a spiritual activity distinct from that of the mechanism and its working. In fact finality is not outside mechanical and efficient causes, but is within their harmony, their order and their unity. This applies to the universe, for there the causes which can explain the evolution of beings only obey an immanent thought, and therefore, far from accounting for the order of the world, presuppose it.

7. *Conclusion. The scientific arguments.* These, then, are the metaphysical proofs for the existence of God. All, as we have seen, start from experience, and conclude to the existence of God as the only possible and adequate explanation of this experience. Their somewhat technical form should not conceal that the task of them all is to render explicit an intuition, namely, the strong rational feeling we have that the world is not self-explanatory, but demands a transcendent cause. This intuition often takes the following form: if there is a moment when nothing exists, nothing will ever exist, but in fact something exists: the universe and all that it contains. Thus there has always been something, and there exists a necessary being. Is this necessary being distinct from the world or not? Ultimately that is the only question. For we can see that the existence of God is grasped in an intuitive way as in some sense evident, and to this extent there are no atheists. The only problem is to know if this God, who is necessary and plainly exists, is the same as the universe, or transcends the universe.

We can regard this problem as already solved by the arguments which have led us to God, for the act of knowing the existence of God is also a knowledge of his nature. God's nature is impressed upon our reason, the more so in proportion to our progress, as that of an infinite and infinitely perfect being, the universal cause of all that is, pure act, absolutely transcending the whole universe. In short, I have only to sum up the results of the argument. Since, however, a number of special difficulties have been put forward by philosophers about the nature of God, I shall deal separately and fully with this question.

Before beginning this, however, I think a few words, in the shape of an appendix, should be said about what have been called the scientific proofs for the existence of God. The proofs just explained which, in a more or less detailed form, are common to the whole spiritual tradition of the west, are certainly, in the strictest sense, scientific proofs. They are based on reality, grasped by experience, and follow the rigorous logic which all true science follows, in contrast to mere opinion or the irrational movement of feeling. Yet, with the immense development of natural science or positive science, it has become customary to keep the word science for these disciplines, to distinguish them from philosophy, though this is, at least by right, as perfectly a science as the positive sciences, but in a different way. Consequently, when a man speaks of "scientific demonstrations" of the existence of God, he refers to proofs of God which would be provided by natural science itself, and which would also, as thereby implied, have the positive character (that is, from experience) which belongs to them. Thus the question is: do such proofs exist, and what is their value; that is, while scientific in form are they also scientific in the rigour of their reasoning?

These scientific demonstrations of God were very numerous in the seventeenth century, when they were put forward in a mathematical form, and in the nineteenth century, when they were based rather on physical science. I shall confine myself to the latter, for the mathematical proofs (defended by

Descartes, who gives in a geometric form—*more geometrico* —a summary of the arguments in support of the existence of God, especially those of Morin, Spinoza and Leibniz) can only argue *a priori,* in so far at least as they are really mathematical. They are composed of definitions, axioms and theorems, which only aim at breaking up the concepts and propositions into their simple elements (in particular by analysis of the concept of infinite being, or of the idea of being). They are exposed, however, to the decisive objection made against the ontological argument in its classical form, which was explained above.

Among the proofs taken from physical science, I will mention that which has been most often employed, and which is based on the principle of entropy of Clausius. He declares that "the energy of the universe is constant and the entropy of the universe (that is, the quantity of heat contained in a body divided by its absolute degree of temperature) tends towards a maximum". The argument, when set out, comes to this. In virtue of the principle of entropy, all the energy of nature tends to transform itself into heat (or calorific energy), and this heat itself tends to reach a final stable equilibrium which would render organic life impossible. Now, in view of the fact that uniform dispersal of energy has not yet come about (because organic life still exists), we must admit that the world is not infinite in time (or eternal), and that it had a beginning. For if it was infinite in time, whatever the quantity of energy it possessed, the equilibrium, destructive of all organic life, would of necessity have already been realized. Hence the world had a beginning. But if it had a beginning, this can only be explained by the creative action of a first cause, which must be God. Thus God exists.

In spite of its apparent rigour, this argument is unsound. For: 1. It implies the postulate that the universe is a closed and finite system. But this postulate is very debatable, since we cannot, by right or in fact, exclude *a priori* the hypothesis that the universe is infinite in extension, and hence possesses an amount of energy which is naturally infinite. This of itself prevents us from affirming either beginning or end to the universe with certainty and in the name of positive science. 2. The very principle of the argument may be called in question. It consists in supposing that we could reach an absolute beginning by regression in the series of coordinate causes. But we have seen that this method must be rejected, since, in the order of temporal succession there is nothing to prevent our going to infinity. 3. Finally and in particular, ultimate origins are necessarily outside the scope of positive science, that is, experience. We have no positive means (from experience) for transcending the totality of the world. Experience of a genesis of the world is self-contradictory. To science the universe is a datum, and nothing more. All it can do is to lead us to raise problems which it cannot solve by its own means. Thus this discussion shows that philosophic rigour must demand more even than "scientific" rigour.

At the present day it is biology especially, in the persons of Alexis Carrel and Lecomte du Nouty, that has been called upon to give a scientific demonstration of God's existence. But there has been no more success than with the demonstrations from physical science or mathematical proofs. Whatever its form, positive science, which is of its very definition a knowledge of the world and of its phenomena, cannot have any metaphysical scope. The proposed demonstrations of God either make a secret (and unskilful) appeal to principles of philosophic and rational order, or else go beyond what science as such can do. In either case, they have the grave disadvantage of letting it be thought that the existence of God can be established under the form of an equation or of a datum of experience. Further, by discrediting by implication the true arguments, which must be rational and metaphysical, they offer, by their sophistic character, too easy a target for negative criticism.

On the other hand I must also point out that all the arguments which some scholars (for example, Einstein, not to mention Marxists, whose negative theories are remarkably weak) offer against the existence of God, have not, and cannot have, any true application. Science as such can prove nothing, in the strict sense, either for or against God. Its business is to explore, and describe the world of phenomena and to discover its most general laws, gathering these together, if possible, in a unity. It cannot go beyond this, because its methods and its means of investigation are, in the nature of the case, within the domain of sense. In fact all the negative arguments which can be advanced from the scientific standpoint, amount to saying with Cabanis (1757-1808) that no instrument has ever succeeded in finding in man the presence of spirit, nor in the world the presence of God. This, however, means nothing, since, if they exist, neither the spiritual soul nor God are things that can be reached by means of a scalpel, or touched by the sense or any apparatus which extends the scope of the senses and is only a more refined sense. To know God other means than those of positive science are absolutely necessary, and in the end it all depends on man's reason, a metaphysical organ and instrument, which allows us to go beyond the world of phenomena, and to grasp, together with being and its universal laws, the very principle of being and the final reason of the whole.

CHAPTER III

THE NATURE OF GOD

I. THE DIVINE ATTRIBUTES

1. *Deduction of the attributes.* I begin by putting together the notions we have formed about God in the course of this inquiry, so that we may understand all that they imply with regard to the divine nature or the divine attributes.

We have shown that God is necessarily incorporeal, because he is essentially one, while corporeal being is, on the contrary, multiple, at least potentially, that is, so far as it is capable of division.

God is perfectly simple, for otherwise he would be, as are all composite things, posterior (at least logically) to his component parts. He would not then be absolutely first, as the universal principle must be.

God is absolutely perfect and infinite, since, possessing his being by his very essence, he possesses it necessarily, without restriction or limit.

Therefore God is necessarily present everywhere, since he is the universal principle, and everything exists and acts through him.

God is utterly unchangeable, since he is pure act, the unmoved principle of all that "becomes", the perfect fullness of being.

God is eternal, because nothing of that which begins to be is pure act, or absolutely first principle, or perfectly unchangeable being, or being of itself. Everything which begins to exist is dependent on another being, who causes it to exist. The eternity of God is the possession, total and perfect, of a life without limitation. Thus it is an unchangeable present, which coexists with all times.

God is sovereign thought and reason, for, being pure spirit, and excluding on this account not only all matter but also all potency, he necessarily contains and embraces the absolute totality of all that is or can be. Hence God of himself knows himself perfectly, and as source and principle of universal being he knows all being, and he does so in and by his own essence as participated in, or able to be participated in, by the beings he calls or can call into existence.

God is life, in the sense that all that is in him is constantly in act and excludes all potency. Thus he is infinite life. God has in himself absolutely the beginning and end of all his activity, while nothing moves him from outside. He possesses himself absolutely, fully and eternally. This divine life is, properly speaking, the act of intelligence, for, as Aristotle says, "the act of intelligence is a life and God is actuality, that is, the very fullness of intelligence; the essential activity of God is perfect and eternal life. We say, then, that God is a living being, eternal and perfect. Thus eternal life belongs to God, for that is what God is."[1]

God, living and eternal, is endowed with will, and with a will which is absolutely free, from the fact that he is absolutely first, and which can only determine itself in conformity with his intelligence, which is himself. Further, the divine will is almighty, because God, being absolutely first and universal principle of all being, can find nothing outside himself to limit his being or his power.

God is love, because, being free to act and to create, he can only act and create through pure, free, generosity, that is, through love. He is also perfect goodness and beauty, the principle and model of all that has any beauty and goodness.

God is providence, because the order of things cannot be separated from the things themselves, and because he who

---

[1] Aristotle, *Metaphysics*, 1072 b, 28.

creates through love can only have the feeling of a father for his handiwork.

2. *Analogy*. This is how we speak of God, describing what tradition calls "the divine names". Nevertheless, as St Thomas constantly repeats, we know nothing of God, or at least we can do nothing more than stammer, and our knowledge of God can only be fully defended by the negative act of saying what God is not.

For, as we have seen, God absolutely transcends the universe. St John Damascene calls him "an ocean of substance without determination of limit", and adds, "it is impossible to say what God is in himself, and it is more accurate to refer to him by denying everything in regard to him. He is not among those things which exist. This does not mean that he exists in no way (since he is the supreme being; he who is), but he is beyond everything which exists, and beyond being itself." That is why negation must accompany all our affirmations, not only because we must deny of God all that is incompatible with his infinite perfection (such as matter and body or senses, which imply in themselves essential imperfection), but also because none of the perfections we attribute to God belong to him in the sense or in the mode in which they belong to creatures. Plainly God, as first principle of universal being, possesses all that is positive in the order of finite perfections, but he possesses it in the accepted phrase, *eminently*, that is, in a strictly infinite degree and without any of the limits which inevitably accompany our own perfections. If, for example, we say that God is thought, we must add at once that he is not a thought like ours, which acts by discourse and reasoning and uses abstract concepts. The divine mind or thought acts in a manner radically different from ours, without discourse, concept, or movement. And we must admit that even this is not to grasp the divine thought adequately. Infinitely surpassing our human modes of knowledge, it escapes all our attempts to grasp it in itself. Even when we raise to the height of the absolute all the positive perfection we have, we only succeed in giving a more precise and definite form to our ignorance. Our ignorance then becomes, in a famous phrase of St Augustine, an ignorance which is aware of itself, *docta ignorantia*.

All this expresses what is called the method of analogy, of which the fundamental principle is that we can establish a true relation (or relation of proportion) between beings, when one possesses a perfection in the true and perfect sense, and others in a secondary and limited sense. It is this proportion which forms a basis for argument about God, and gives it meaning. Thus, when we say that God is good, we mean that there is a certain relation or proportion between the essential goodness of God, and the imperfect and varied goodness which we practise in our human world. It is also this proportion which shows us our inability to speak adequately of God, since it implies that the absolute terms of the relation, for example God's goodness, is *essentially different* from our goodness. Hence we can see that our knowledge of God can only be true when affirmation is accompanied by negation: the two go together and are inseparable. The "wise ignorance" of St Augustine, which I have just referred to, implies nothing else than this. By this means we can escape both from agnosticism, which means that we can know absolutely nothing about God, neither whether he exists nor what he is, and from anthropomorphism, which applies to God human attributes in their deficient and imperfect mode.

It must be admitted, however, that, when we think or speak of God, we cannot be free from a certain anthropomorphism from the very fact that we must necessarily appeal to concepts and images derived from our experience. But an anthropomorphism which is aware of itself at once corrects itself, at least so far as it can. Moreover we should go too far if we denied all validity and all usefulness to this imperfect manner of thinking about God, because it gives a necessary starting point to our thought which is not that of an angel but of a man. However gross and wretched the images may be, they

are a help to the man who denies them while using them. If
we know they are fallacious we thereby avoid the inadequacy
and limitation of our thought.

3. *Immanence and transcendence*. What I have just said
would be all that is strictly required, if difficulties, raised
especially by modern philosophy, did not force us to examine
more carefully the problem which may be called that of the
divine personality.

We must agree that pantheism represents one of the tendencies into which the human mind slips most easily, on
account of the partial truth it contains, as I shall explain later
on. If, generally speaking, religions, using the word in its
strict sense, have only very rarely admitted pantheistic ideas,
but on the contrary have supported personalist, indeed anthro-
pomorphic, notions of the divinity, strictly philosophic
thought has often shown strong tendencies towards pantheism,
and has sometimes tried to give a systematic and coherent
form to pantheism. A great thinker of the present day, though
formally a theist (that is, professing the personal nature of an
absolutely transcendent God, the creator of the universe),
even declared (but wrongly) that "philosophy is essentially
pantheist", and that it is Christian faith alone which reveals
to us the personality of God. Lao-Tse, with his *tao* or primordial principle, unity which is also the whole, Brahmanism,
with its pantheistic syncretism, the Neoplatonism of Plotinus
with its conception of emanation, the medieval theories of
Averroës, David of Dinant (for whom God is prime matter),
Giordano Bruno, and then, in modern times, the philosophies
of Spinoza, Schleiermacher, Fichte and Hegel, mark different
stages and varieties of a doctrine of which the essential theme
can be expressed in the two following forms: either "God
alone is real; the world is only a collection of manifestations
or emanations having neither reality nor distinct substance",
or "the world alone is real; God is only the sum of all that
exists". The first form is represented mainly by the doctrines
of Plotinus and Spinoza; the second is that of materialistic

pantheism, of which Marxism seems to be the type. In both it can be said that all is God, that the world and God make up but one thing.

That which gives force to pantheism, and provides it with its continued power to seduce is the deep feeling, which animates it, of God's *immanence* in everything that exists. For it is very true, as shown by what I have already said, that God, being necessarily the first principle, universal cause, must be present in everything that exists, and must even be more closely present to things than they are to themselves since they only exist and subsist as a result of a continual influx of creative power. Nothing is truer than what St Paul says: "in God we live, and move and have our being". Hence pantheism is based on insistence on the depth and universality of the divine immanence. Its error, however, lies in underestimating or even denying God's transcendence, that is, God's absolute independence in relation to the world, in failing to understand that we must conceive him by analogy (and to use the words of Leibniz) as being "what a designer is to his machine, what a prince is to his subjects, and even what a father is to his children". For the divine transcendence means, if we grasp all its implications, the doctrine of creation, that is, the free production by God of all that exists, and consequently it means the reality in God of an infinite intelligence and will.

All this necessarily follows from the arguments which have led us to assert the existence of God. Nevertheless it should not and cannot make us deny or underestimate God's immanence, which follows with equal necessity. Immanence and transcendence are two aspects, both unavoidable, of an idea of God which is in conformity with the demands of experience as well as those of reason. Unless immanent, God is a stranger to the universe and is neither infinite nor perfect: the idea of God becomes contradictory. Unless transcendent, God becomes identical with the universe, and again appears as imperfect, potential, in a state of becoming, and the notion of God is no less contradictory than in the first case. To tell the truth, in each there is an implicit denial of God, so that, as Malebranche points out, all pantheism amounts to a kind of atheism.

What is essential here is to understand rightly the meaning of transcendence and immanence. Our difficulties usually come from a fatal habit of imagining things spatially. Neither immanence nor transcendence are represented or rendered by images, since they are not of the material order, and, as I have said, the divine essence and attributes take us to the infinite. Thus transcendence does not mean beyond space, but essentially an absolute independence, a total self-sufficiency, a perfect aseity (aseity being the property of that which exists of itself, and in virtue of itself). Immanence, again, is not a vague mingling of the divine being with created things. Before his conversion St Augustine fell into this error, of which he speaks in a moving passage of his *Confessions*, which I must quote. Addressing God, he writes:

> So also did I endeavour to conceive of this, Life of my life, as vast, through infinite spaces, on every side penetrating the whole mass of the universe, and beyond it, every way, through unmeasurable boundless spaces; so that the earth should have Thee, the heaven have Thee, all things have Thee, and they be bounded in Thee, and Thou bounded nowhere. For that as the body of this air which is above the earth, hindereth not the light of the sun from passing through it, penetrating it, not by bursting or by cutting, but by filling it wholly: so I thought the body not of heaven, air and sea only, but of the earth too, pervious to Thee, so that in all its parts, the greatest as the smallest, it should admit Thy presence, by a secret inspiration, within and without, directing all things which Thou hast created. So I guessed, only as unable to conceive aught else, for it was false. For thus should a greater part of the earth contain a greater portion of Thee, and a less, a lesser: and all things should in such sort be full of Thee, that the body of an elephant should contain more of Thee than that of a sparrow, by how much larger it is, and takes up more room; and thus

shouldest Thou make the several portions of Thyself present
unto the several portions of the world, in fragments, large to
the large, petty to the petty. But such art not Thou. But not as
yet hadst Thou enlightened my darkness.[1]

From this darkness and this mass of contradictions St
Augustine emerged, when he understood that the divine
immanence could only be a mode of *spiritual presence,* not
reducible to bodily presence, and hence infinitely more inti-
mate, penetrating and close.

However, we must examine the pantheistic conception in
more detail, because it is the crucial point in the problem of
God. This examination will also be a confirmation or proof
of the conclusions we have already reached. We shall see that
they really imply the certitude and the demands on our reason
with regard to God's nature, which we believe we have found
in them.

II. *PANTHEISM*

1. *The logic of transcendence.* Even pantheists, as I have
already said, think we should attribute a certain transcendence to God: there must be some kind of distinction between
God and the universe, or else to assert God's existence can
only be a matter of words. Plotinus and Spinoza in particular
are in agreement about this. We may take it, then, as a
starting point, if discussion with a pantheist is to lead anywhere, especially as it is to experience that we wish to appeal.
For the analysis of moral consciousness, quite as much as
that of intellectual consciousness, makes us acknowledge
that, as transitory individuals, we are in a sense plunged into
a reality which precedes us and survives us, passes through
us and beyond us, is our principle of life and of movement to
higher things. A basic will to live which perpetuates the life
of the family and of the species, an ever increasing urge
towards reasonableness and justice, a realization of know-

[1] St Augustine, *Confessions,* Bk. 7, trans. E. B. Pusey.

ledge and science, of morality and religion, never final but pursued with tireless perseverance, an irresistible tendency towards spiritual perfection, ever renewing itself in spite of apparent checks: so do these deep waters appear, of which we, poor individuals on the surface of being, are scarcely perceptible eddies.

Now this kind of intuition of the life force introduces us, so to speak, to immanence; it permits us to plunge for a moment into the heart of the real and of the divine, of that divine of which we are, but of which we are not all. That is what Lachelier tried to say in the passage quoted above about the "pantheistic" character of pure philosophy. But, at the same time, this intuition includes the sense or idea of a transcendence, for the distinction between the divine and the world is only one of words without meaning unless we admit the transcendence of the divine. Without transcendence, without a certain independence on the part of the divine, are we not led to think that the distinction between God and the world is, in some way or other, but a mere abstraction without foundation in reality?

Nor is it any help to say that the divine is a kind of force or urge within phenomena or experience. For if we are concerned with an inwardness which excludes all transcendence, that is, which excludes an existence absolutely independent in relation to the universe, the divine will appear, says Parodi, as "on the same level as experience, one of its elements, one of its parts, and hence incapable of explaining the whole from which it is taken". This is a very pregnant remark, which shows clearly that the pantheistic explanation involves a vicious circle, being ultimately nothing else than an explanation of a thing by means of itself. To explain the universe, though we need not go outside it (for we cannot do this), we must grasp in the universe itself a transcendence which both dwells in it and goes beyond it; true immanence demands genuine transcendence, no *part* of the whole being able, of its very meaning, to be present to the whole as such. Only that which transcends the whole can be present to the whole. Hence there is not really divine immanence in the universe, unless God transcends this universe.

2. *The logic of experience.* Most pantheistic theories have, at root, seen all this fairly clearly. But the difficulty in which pantheists are involved is that they do in fact compromise this divine transcendence, which they yet regard as necessary. What, then, is required by a real transcendence? Manifestly, I repeat once more, there can be no question of a spatial conception, of an exteriority which would make nonsense of divine immanence. But bodily things are necessarily external to one another. Hence the divine principle is *spiritual in its nature,* for only spirit or what is analogous to spirit, transcends space and time, and, moreover, only spirit can explain the existence of finite thoughts, reason and morality. "God", wrote Lagneau, "not only creates everything, but produces, creates, thought itself." So we cannot conceive him as "*a natura naturans* who exists by the mere necessity of nature, who exists purely and simply (Spinoza): such a necessity cannot produce thought. How can we suppose that from this nature should flow thought and the infinite diversity of beings?"[1]

Moreover, we must have a right idea of this spiritual principle and its transcendence. Very often pantheism, in contradiction with its own principles, falls far short of what is required by a consistent assertion of transcendence. It shows very pertinently that the divine, appearing as foundation and source of all existence and of all activity, must necessarily be distinct from all that it realizes, and distinct through something essential. But what is meant here by "essential"? It means, if we are to be consistent, a *difference of nature.* Strictly speaking pantheism grants this consequence, but it does not drive home the admission to its strict, logical, end.

[1] J. Lagneau, *Célèbres leçons*, p. 262. By *natura naturans* Spinoza means the world itself as infinite substance.

The pantheist often puts God in opposition to the world, as subject to object, as the act of thinking to the content of the thought. He notices that by the duplicating process of reflection the subject can make itself its own object indefinitely, or, conversely, discover itself as a possible constituent in each of its objects. All reality, in this conception of idealist pantheism, is thus reduced to a Thought (God) which thinks itself (the universe). Now there is undoubtedly an important truth in this doctrine, namely, the assertion that there exists a Thought, distinct from all individual thoughts which are finite and passing, a Thought which subsists otherwise and more eminently than ourselves as individuals, and which affirms its presence in and through rational, spiritual and moral demands, with numberless implications, made upon the infinite and independent powers of the activity of the individual judgement. Outside of space and time, and in a way which is infinitely beyond our imagination, this Thought must have truth and reality. It is precisely this important truth which is brought forward by the argument from the degrees of being and the eternal truths.

But under what exact conditions has it truth and reality? Will it still preserve them if we suppose, as does pantheism, that the numberless multitude of empirical and distinct thoughts, of individual acts of knowing, which yet are affirmed in and for themselves, are nothing else than pure objects or contents of Thought, that is, are a mere *representation*? If Thought reflects on itself and takes itself for object indefinitely, the object is then only distinct from the subject by abstraction, and the universe of Thought is nothing else than Thought itself (Sartre, we can see, is caught in this difficulty). On the one hand there is no essential difference, no difference of nature, between Thought and the objects thought, though this is contrary to what we have seen to be necessary. On the other hand, and as a result of this, the transcendence of Thought is purely illusory, quite apart from the fact that the in-itself and for-itself of the individual acts of thought, that is, of the thinking subjects which we are, becomes unintelligible. This is a point which a contemporary thinker, Octave Hamelin, has emphasized, showing that pantheism leads to the double contradiction of positing an "unconscious thought" and a "single individual". For, he says, the concept of an "unconscious thought" can have no meaning, because thought belongs to mind, that is, to a being who is necessarily consciousness, namely, consciousness both of his own thought and hence also of himself. We must say the same, adds Hamelin, of the notion of an "impersonal thought", which involves the same contradiction. Then, since pantheism leads to the conception of the totality of being as a single individual (Plotinus held this, saying that the universe was like "a great animal") it runs against the fact that there are many centres of consciousness. "If we establish that there are many centres of consciousness, pantheism is unacceptable, for a consciousness is individual, it is a being."[1]

Here we see one of the reasons which make it necessary to reject pantheism entirely. If Thought only thinks the beings we experience and especially beings which are subjects, that is, which are conscious and which think, if it only thinks of these as pure objects and as a mere immanent content, how have these beings the conviction of being in themselves and for themselves, how do they know themselves, and think themselves and affirm themselves as real and distinct from the universe or the whole; how do they come to regard themselves as personal beings, free and responsible? To turn the argument round, if there are in the universe persons, subjects, who are clearly and distinctly aware of themselves and in the most formal manner, as reasonable, free and autonomous, they must necessarily be distinct from Thought (or God), that is, to speak more accurately, Thought (or God) in establishing them, gives them a reality of their own, which is not identical with his.

[1] O. Hamelin, *Essai sur les éléments principaux de la représentation*, pp. 451-2.

Here, however, I must mention a view, sometimes appealed to by Christian thinkers, and which seems to contradict the above ideas. Pantheism, it is said, is true at least in one instance, that of Christ, the Man-God, and consequently most refutations of pantheism prove nothing because they try to prove too much. It seems to me impossible to subscribe to this way of presenting the mystery of the Incarnation, which, at least so far as it is offered for our belief by Christian faith, has absolutely no connection with pantheism. For, in the Incarnation, the hypostatic union formally implies the distinction of *two natures,* the divine nature and the human nature, which remain, even when united in the unity of a single person, irreducible to one another. Pantheism, on the other hand, implies unity of nature. Again, the Incarnation excludes duality of persons (the single person is that of the Son of God), while, in pantheism, the plurality of empirical persons, with all the properties inalienable from free, autonomous and responsible subjects, is both demanded in fact (unless it is to have no meaning at all for pantheism), and unintelligible for reason. Consequently the two cannot be compared at all. Finally, in the Incarnation the human nature of Christ is itself *created,* just as are all other individual human natures, and the transcendence of God remains absolute in regard to this nature assumed by the Divinity, and here again an infinite distance is put between this mystery and pantheism.

Thus, after showing the inconsistency of a pantheism "in which, as always happens, the very God whom we think we see everywhere, in the end has not existence anywhere",[1] we can conclude that the assertions are valid to which the proofs of the existence of God have led us. Every other conception of God conceals incoherences and contradictions which end in compromising either the immanence or the transcendence of God. We have seen that both of these are plainly necessary

---

[1] L. Lavelle, *De l'âme humaine,* p. 522.

to express, so far as is possible, and with the help of analogy, the mysterious reality of the divine Being.

III. *THE DIVINE PERSONALITY*

1. *God is a personal Being.* We must agree, then, that God, if he exists, can only be the infinite being, fundamentally distinct from the universe which he has created and which he keeps in being by an act of free will, and consequently that God is a being whom we call, by analogy with that which we know and experience in ourselves, *personal,* that is, subsistent, intelligent and free. As I have shown above, in agreement with Descartes, Lagneau and Hamelin, it is incredible that the principle from which proceed in the universe the free, intelligent, subjects which we are, souls thirsting for truth, justice and beauty, as we can and should become, that this principle is some impersonal reality, unconscious, and obedient to a kind of inward necessity, a law which determines it. This would involve an impossible contradiction.

Nevertheless, plainly God is not a personal being such as we are. Being pure spirit he has no body; intelligence and will in him are not what they are in us. Further, those properties which define personality in us, intelligence, will, freedom, are not really distinct from the divine being, for God is subsistent Intelligence, and subsistent Will. All the distinctions which the poverty of our language and the limitations of our reason compel us to make in our speech about God, are in him only virtual distinctions, based on the infinite richness of his essence, but transformed by our conceptual thought into real multiplicity. God passes beyond us to an infinite degree. Yet in spite of all this we can have some knowledge of this infinite. For, as rational free subjects, we are persons, even though petty persons subject to so many limitations. Now though it is true that the only personal existences that we experience are our human existences, we can, nevertheless, in knowing ourselves, conceive up to a certain point a personal life without the representation of a living body. For we are quite aware that the body, far from constituting the personality, is itself a kind of limitation and obstacle to it, while at the same time a means for it to act. From one point of view the body is that which enslaves us to the world of things, that which limits our expansion, confines our field of action, and acts as a brake on our voluntary activity. Indeed we are clearly aware of only becoming ourselves, of possessing ourselves, when we abound in the sense of our spiritual being, just as, on the other hand, it is in the degree in which they become more material that beings sink into impersonality. In short, spirit is the definition of personality. If, then, God is essentially spirit, he is essentially personal.

This is another reason for us to reject pantheism still more definitely. For if God is confounded with the universe, he cannot be a personal being, that is, a being for himself. In whatever way the attempt is made to give a look of consistency to this conception, the God-Universe, or Universe-God, is a composite and multiple being, a being who makes himself and unmakes himself, a series which never reaches an end, a potency, the perfect act of which is never given, an addition sum which is never completed, while personality necessarily, of its very meaning, implies inward unity, possession of self, and, if we refer to God, that fullness and that perfection of understanding and freedom which has been called pure act.

2. *God is love.* It should be added, in conformity with the light which reason owes to the Christian revelation, but which the paganism of old (among others in Plato) had only caught a glimpse of, that God is love, and that he is subsistent love. Of course, here again, anthropomorphism is both a help and a danger. It helps us to think of the divine love, but at the same time makes us tend to give that love the form of our own love. When we say that God is love, there is no question of conceiving him as subject to that passion which is connected in our humanity, being sensible, with bodily

phenomena, troubles and restlessness. Plainly God cannot experience movements of desire and anger, which in us result from the deprivation and absence of what we desire, or from the presence of what we dread. Divine love knows no passivity, because it is pure act and absolute fruitfulness. God, who, as we have seen, knows, in and through his essence, the numberless beings he could call into existence as so many participations of his essence, loves all these beings as so many images more or less distant from himself, and when he brings them into existence by creation, this only results from his love. For it is the property of love to give out of pure generosity and without thought of self. God gives, and gives himself, because he is infinite love, as he is infinite being.

Pagan philosophers, such as Aristotle, were not able to raise their conception of God to these heights and, in order to safeguard the immutability of pure act, thought that God must have no knowledge of the world. Aristotle, however, fully realized that God must be the first source of all movement of nature, and in particular of our aspirations for the good, the beautiful and the one. The whole universe, as he finely expressed it, depends upon the first mover. But since a more exact exercise of reason, clarified and supported by Christian revelation, has led us to the idea of creation, how can we do otherwise than refer to God, as to their source, all the inward movements which bring us to virtue, service of our neighbour, charity and justice, as well as all our aspirations for the assured and lasting possession of the absolute good? How can we do otherwise than suppose that the creator of the universe, who is the first mover of our hearts as he is the first mover of the world, "he who moves the sky and the stars" (Dante), must himself have, if we may use the words, a heart attentive to our love, and must be truly, in another phrase of Dante, "the first love"?

On this matter Plato had a surer intuition than Aristotle, for when he works out the dialectic of the Symposium, he seems to glimpse the truth that to love is at once to love God, and that all love, through the illimitable urge, the absolute demands, which it implies, is a kind of proof from experience of the existence of a being who is supremely lovable and supremely loving. The world is unintelligible without God, but there is something still more unintelligible, namely, a God who remains fundamentally a stranger to the universe, solely occupied with presiding over the revolutions of the spheres lost in the immensity of space, a God who is a geometer and who is ignorant of those other revolutions in the universe, incomparably more beautiful than the movements of the stars, those of our souls round the centre of light and love. Thus we have a profound conviction that our aspirations for absolute good and justice can only have meaning if they tend towards a personal being, whose watchful love sees into the secret rhythm of our hearts. The dreadful solitude of infinite space and its silence, of which Pascal speaks, cannot end in a mere sense of the existence of a nameless energy, diffused throughout the universe. For what we desire, with an unalterable will, which is a second nature to us, and even in a sense our true nature, since it is above all by the spirit that we can act, is the firm, lasting and personal possession of the absolute good. That is why men only find peace, and thought only finds true intelligibility in the certitude of the existence of a God who is both infinite thought and infinite love. That is the whole of what Augustine meant by a famous sentence, when he said to God: "Our hearts can find no peace till they rest in thee".

IV. *CREATION AND PROVIDENCE*

1. *The creation of the world.* The creation of the universe by God is implied in all that has just been said. It is not, therefore, the fact of creation which is being discussed here, but only the manner of creation. Plainly I am speaking of creation in the strictest sense, that is, of the absolute production of universal being by God, or of what tradition calls

creation out of nothing. But we must notice at once that our language, here again but especially here, only serves our thought very inadequately. For, on the one hand, the term "production" suggests a kind of putting together, which is clearly inapplicable to the divine act of creation. This is not exercised upon a pre-existing material, as are our human acts of production, but causes to arise, together and absolutely, the matter and the infinitely varied forms of the world. On the other hand, it is also inaccurate to say "creation out of nothing" (*ex nihilo*), for "nothing" being simply nothing (not-being has no kind of existence) cannot be a starting point or a presupposition for the divine creative activity. To these difficulties which arise from our way of expressing ourselves, must be added those which are due to the imagination, and which lead us to think that creation implies a beginning in time. This is false, because creation in its essence completely abstracts from a temporal beginning. Creation, in the absolute sense, only means the absolute dependence of the universe not only in its being (or existence) but also in its whole content, in relation to God.

From this point of view, which is that of natural reason, we have to say that creation can and indeed must be thought of as outside time, not only on God's side, as is manifest, since God, being pure act, is not subject to time but is eternal, but also on the creature's side. I have already emphasized this point, in my general review of the metaphysical proofs. It is sufficient, then, to repeat here, that to assert that the world is created does not mean that the world began in time, that is to, say, to be more precise, that from the moment of creation a finite time (however long) has passed. Nor does it mean the opposite. I say simply that the world does not exist of itself, nor in virtue of itself, but that it proceeds absolutely and wholly from God and from an act of his sovereign freedom.

Undoubtedly the creative activity, understood in this way, infinitely surpasses our finite thought. We only understand adequately what we can do ourselves. But here we are in the realm of God's infinite power. Yet, our inability to understand creation is no reason for denying it: creation is one of those "necessary hypotheses" (that is, such that, without them, everything becomes meaningless) which are equivalent to the most invincible of certitudes. For to deny the reality of creation, in the sense I have explained, amounts to asserting the aseity of the universe: it amounts to saying that the universe exists of itself, in virtue of its very nature, and hence that it is God. With such a conception, to claim still to leave a place, so to speak, for God as distinct from the universe is a desperate attempt. If the world exists of itself, God must be limited by the world; there is being, apart from God, which is outside his power. Thus God is neither infinite nor almighty, that is, if we are consistent, God is not God. Sheer contradiction follows, complete incoherence. Hence, if creation is a mystery to us, it is at least a mystery which throws light on everything else. To deny creation multiplies enigmas, and leads us to absurdities. On the one hand it implies atheism, and on the other hand lays down that the world, which appears as an essentially imperfect being, has in itself the perfect reason for its existence. Descartes, as we have seen, dealt with this palpable error.

Sartre, however, is not convinced. He asserts that creation *ex nihilo* is meaningless, and that it is better to admit the thorough absurdity of the world, that is, to admit that the world exists without any reason and is "superfluous for eternity". Must we stop to examine these paradoxes, which propose the suicide of reason? After all I have said, it might seem useless to do so, but the wide diffusion of these extreme theories makes a short discussion necessary. Sartre's theory amounts to the following two arguments: (1) Creation *ex nihilo* cannot explain the emergence of being, because universal being must (*ex hypothesi*) be first conceived by the divine subjectivity, and for this reason remains an intrasubjective mode of being, without leaving room for a mere representation of a possible objectivity, or therefore for a will to create being. (2) In fact this will is inconceivable because it can only be exercised effectively in producing being which, when created, would necessarily escape the creator "in order at once to be enclosed in itself and assume its being", that is, the creature would present itself as an absolute, which was autonomous and independent: God in creating would deny and destroy himself.

The first point to make in reply to these arguments is that they are a sheer refusal to admit the idea of creation, but no proof of its impossibility. For, (1) to say that universal being can only be conceived by God as a subjective mode of being, but not thought of as realizable (or as able to be objectivized), is at once to introduce contradiction. If God conceives universal being, that is to say (and otherwise we can say nothing), the world of creatures, he must necessarily conceive it as realizable, for how otherwise could he conceive it precisely as a world of creatures? By analogy we see that, when a man conceives a work, he conceives it at the same time as "doable". (2) But Sartre denies that our experience is valid here precisely because, if we apply it to God analogically, it leads to supposing a world created independently of God (just as, when we "create" something, the thing produced, once produced, is independent of us, and is "opposed to" the producer). This argument, as we can see, is the result of pure anthropomorphism, and asserts of God what is only true of man. If we are exact, man does not "create"; he changes things which subsist without him, and in a sense "contrary to" him (that is, over against him). God, on the other hand, creates in the absolute sense, which implies that the created being, incapable of existing by itself, when once created continues to receive the creative inflow, and consequently neither limits God nor is opposed to him. That is why we express ourselves badly when we speak of being "once created" since, if we are accurate, creation does not cease, and the being only exists and subsists by this continued creation—even "continuation" being only our way of thinking of creation as an event in time, while on God's side creation is a timeless act which includes in its unity the whole duration of created being. The creative act is precisely coextensive with all the successive reality of the world.

Thus we can see that creation, far from implying the independence of the world in relation to God, implies on the contrary essentially and at every moment the complete dependence of the world in its very being. It is nothing else than the continual renewing of this relation to God which is the very definition of the creative act. Hence we are right in saying that on every hypothesis (that is, that the world has had or has not had a beginning in time), it is essential to the world to be always beginning, since its moments only succeed one another and are connected together by the creative power of God. To begin is, for it, the absolute corollary of its metaphysical weakness. This was seen clearly by Descartes when he assumed that at every moment the world became nothing, and was created every moment by God. This was only his way of conveying the absolute contingency of the universe, and the character, coextensive with all the moments of the world, of the creative act.

That is also why the idea of creation does not at all imply the idea of an empty duration, before concrete duration and real duration and real existence. In this we only find an imaginary form, as such basically false, since it amounts to supposing being before being. Before the universe (whatever may be the meaning of "before"), there is only God's eternity. Time belongs to finite being, which is set by its nature amid succession and becoming. Whether the duration of the world is finite or infinite, time started with it. Universal being, in its substance and in the attributes which affect it, including temporal duration, is produced by an act of God which is absolute and outside time.

2. *Divine Providence.* Creation implies providence, that is, the activity by which God directs the whole universe towards

spiritual ends, which give it its value and its meaning. In fact providence, rightly considered, is identical with the creative activity of God. If we make a distinction between them, this is on account of our very imperfect way of conceiving the divine activity, through which we assume, or rather imagine, a creation completed as a past event and a providence which then is exercised over the work that has been accomplished, just as for example the curator of a museum looks after the works of art under his care.

But this act of imagination, which is inadequate and very defective, does carry with it analogically some truth. For while it is true that the creative act and providence are identified in God, these two activities are logically or virtually distinct, or, if you like, refer to two distinct aspects of a single activity. To create is to produce universal being by an act which is supremely free—and also to exercise providential activity, that is, to bring it about that this creation shall tend constantly and essentially towards the good of creatures. That is why we can speak of divine providence, and then can try to understand, as far as is possible, by what means it is exercised. Nevertheless, it is one thing to assert the reality of this universal providence, and another thing to distinguish the particular ways by which it acts. Reason makes us admit the existence of a providential design which develops gradually and harmoniously throughout the whole history of the world and of the human race. But reason, owing to its limitations, also prevents us from filling in the precise forms of this design, at least as to the details of its development. We can only conceive it by distinguishing in the most general way the mode of the divine government. What else, indeed, do we mean by "providence" than the knowledge of what must be done in order to work towards a given end, and the realization of the plan so determined upon? This amounts to saying that providence belongs both to intelligence and will. We have, then, to look at it in God himself from this twofold point of view.

Here analogy should give us great help, for divine providence answers in some measure to what is most beautiful and most perfect in our human nature, that is, to all the demands of goodness which belong to fatherhood. Leibniz said truly. in a passage already quoted, that God is to us what a father is to his children. Now fatherhood, when it is all that it should be, implies on the part of the father careful foresight, constantly active, for the greatest possible, and the most perfect possible, good of the children he has brought into the world, and the choice of the most appropriate means to carry out this plan of fatherly love. Human foresight, however, is liable to error, and the means to carry out the plan are often beyond our power. Many obstacles stand in the way, and many unforeseen events upset the plan, so that failure, at least in part, is involved in our human state. A father's providence fails on many counts, and especially because it is exercised on beings who are free, at least when they reach the age of reason, and who can spoil the plans for their wellbeing which were originally made.

Divine providence partly resembles our human providence. It is in fact only another name for the fatherhood of God. For God is our father in the highest sense, far more so than are men in relation to their children, since God is the absolute source of being and of life, while human creatures can only transmit a life of which they are not creators. Again, while allowing for the inevitable anthropomorphism of our thought, we can without doubt attribute to God those deep feelings of foresight, care, love and tenderness, which characterize a human fatherhood worthy of the name. The Son of God has himself taught us this, when he taught us to call God "our Father". But, on the other hand, God is creator and absolute principle of all that exists, and of all the movements, even the most passing, of our hearts. Nothing, therefore, can escape his infinite knowledge, nor, consequently, can anything escape his foresight, which is unlimited since it is eternal, and acts, so to speak, at the very moment at which each of the events of the universe, from its beginning to its end, takes place. God knows no obstacle to the sovereign act by which he foresees and arranges all things for the good of his creatures. Everything—absolutely everything in creation—is done for the greatest good of the beings God has created.

How, then, can it be that the good which God, who is an almighty and infinitely wise father, foresees and ordains, is realized, at least so far as we can see, so imperfectly? I will leave aside the problem of evil, which I shall examine later on. Here I shall only consider the notion of divine providence. Now, within these limits, we can again find a profound analogy with the providence of the human father with regard to his children. We have seen that this meets obstacles it cannot surmount. If we eliminate, as incompatible with divine providence, all the obstacles which among men arise from inability to foresee everything, and to carry out everything as foreseen, there remain obstacles which result from the freedom of the children. Should we speak of this kind of obstacle also in connection with the providence of God? In one sense, yes, for God creates free beings, such, that is, that their destiny lies in their own hands, and consequently that they can hamper the design of a loving providence. In another sense, where analogy does not apply, we must say that providence knows no obstacles. For to God there can be no risk, since nothing escapes God's knowledge, nor can there be any free act that cannot be foreseen. The infinite knowledge of God, for the very reason that it is creative, necessarily extends to all free acts performed by creatures. All such acts, which for us represent contingencies limiting our knowledge and power, are embraced by God's providential activity. In other words God, foreseeing (or better, seeing) absolutely all, brings it about that everything, including the failures and faults of creatures, shall be able to serve their good. That man, however, can ultimately escape through his freedom from God's infinite love for his children, is certainly a mystery, but nothing else than the very mystery of human freedom, willed by God and respected by him even when it rebels against him.

Thus we reach a better conception of the ways of divine providence. Manifestly it has no connection with the incalculable play of caprice; on the contrary, having created the world and at the same time (for there is no difference) the laws which govern it and control its development, God does not intervene arbitrarily to modify the course of events. Rather, providence seems to be in conformity with the nature of each creature, underlying its activity, so to speak, not just opposed to it. Providence penetrates this activity and makes use of it for the good of creatures, which is primarily spiritual, all the rest being only a means for the coming of the kingdom of the spirit. This is the true end of the human race, God himself, as the last end of all that is, being included, as it were, in the mediate end, as that which gives it its true and adequate meaning. Providence is everywhere and in everything, in the revolutions of the spheres and in the growth of germs, in life, and in the movement of our hearts, in the aspirations of our souls and in the stirrings of our good will, in decisions of our free choice which can least be foreseen.

It also follows that providence might appear on the surface to do nothing. Yet it would be useless and absurd to look for it outside the course of events. It is immanent in all the events of the universe, and in all the history of the human race. It is reality itself, and the reality of all times, of every moment of time, and of every place. The whole universe, with all that it contains, is but the visible unfolding of that first love, referred to by Dante, as I have already said.

3. *The problem of evil.* Yet doubt seems thrown upon all this by the existence of evil, always the great difficulty we meet in our path towards God. St Augustine, who had been troubled for long by this difficulty, puts it as follows: "If God exists, whence comes evil?" And another voice in him replied: "If God does not exist, whence comes good?" But this twofold question, which in fact is only one, does not solve the problem; it only presents it in all its rigour. We

must begin, then, by trying to understand it, and then see if reflection on God's work and on human nature can furnish some elements of a solution.

Above all we must define the problem as exactly as possible. What we are concerned with is that kind of evil which is not bound up with (or seems not to be bound up with) bodily nature. Plainly bodily nature, from the very fact that it is bodily, even when considered as whole and perfect in its order, is liable to unavoidable failures which, being themselves conditions for good, cannot count as evils in the proper sense. It is natural to man to work for his food, to be subject to disease and death, to ignorance and error. This only means that human nature is not entirely perfect, that it only represents a low degree in the order of being. Undoubtedly it may be supposed that God could preserve man from these natural imperfections, but such a requirement clearly goes beyond what is owing to us from the justice and wisdom of God. In creating man God need only give him a nature sound in its own order, and all the means required to fulfil his destiny, which consists in tending, amid the difficulties and pains inherent in his bodily state, towards the sovereign good. From this point of view we cannot blame absolute evil for the accidental disorders and relative failures of humanity in its efforts for thousands of years to keep nature to its proper ends. It is by this very effort, in spite of obstacles, and often as a result of obstacles, that man little by little reaches his full height in creation, and becomes its king. Nor can we blame absolute evil for the play of cosmic forces which often cause such disasters to mankind, earthquakes, tidal waves, volcanoes, epidemics, and so on. These phenomena are an aspect of the world order, and man, through the power of his genius and the invention of more and more perfect devices, can lessen, if not remove, the terrible results of these cosmic phenomena.

So reason philosophers in face of the problem of evil. Nevertheless, we feel that these arguments remain unconvincing, and are based on a theoretic optimism, rather than a true appreciation of the history of the world. They are concerned with "human nature", taken in the abstract. They apply to a universe conceived as a system of laws working somehow for its own ends, and valid in its own right. Now what is in question is not simply "human nature", but also and more especially individual men, whose real sufferings cannot be comforted or healed by purely theoretic arguments. We know quite well that an earthquake is a result of the cosmic order, but for the multitudes of human beings whom a tidal wave thunders down upon and plunges to death, amid untold sufferings, this phenomenon, however normal and necessary to the geophysicist, is certainly an evil. So too the failures and misfits of evolution which lead, presumably, to the coming of a better world, are real evils, not merely theoretic or apparent, for those who are their victims. Metaphysical optimism, in its attempt to regard all the evils of mankind as relative, is always running against this reality of individual suffering and cannot escape it. "If we look at the advance of the world from this standpoint, which is not that of its progress, but that of its risks and of the efforts which it requires, we soon see, beneath the appearance of security and harmony which the human Adventure shows when looked at from high up, a peculiar kind of cosmos in which evil (not as a matter of accident, which would not be of much consequence, but by the very nature of the system) appears as a necessity in the wake of evolution, and in any quantity and with any gravity".[1]

Above all there are failures of the will, the faults and crimes by which man renounces his moral destiny, and adds immeasurably to the misery of the world. Here we touch on what may be called, in St Augustine's words, *absolute evil*. For sin, being transgression of the moral law, is the essential

[1] P. Teilhard de Chardin, S.J., *Le Phénomène humain* (Paris, Ed. du Seuil, 1955), p. 347. An English translation of this book is in preparation.

disorder, that which, of itself, so far as it can, destroys the spiritual order which alone gives to the world its true meaning.

That is what is meant, strictly speaking, by the problem of evil. What solution can we suggest for it? Can we indeed suggest any real solution? First it should be noticed that we cannot look for the origin and reason of the various particular evils which oppress humanity. To look for these is beyond our power, and answers always remain hypothetical. What we have to consider is physical and moral evil, as such, in its most general aspect, and philosophical reflection can throw some light on this. It shows us, to begin with, that to deny the existence of God and of divine providence, far from solving the problem of evil, can only make it completely insoluble. For, if there were no remedy or compensation for the evils which we endure, the world would be definitely irrational, without meaning, and radically evil. But, if so, how could we understand the physical order which controls it? In particular how could we understand the fact that this human universe, supposedly irrational and given over to evil, contains so much goodness and moral beauty, and is filled with so profound a need for justice and morality that we can find no meaning in it except through this unquenchable aspiration? If God does not exist, says St Augustine, whence comes good?

Yet, however sound they may be, these considerations offer no complete solution to the problem of evil. They only make us agree that there must be a solution. We must account for at least moral evil, and explain, if we can, that deep unhappiness which is caused by our failures, freely committed. Should we doubt this very freedom and ascribe it too to evil? Impossible, reply the philosophers following St Augustine, because liberty, even though it can lead to failure, is a good. It is a wonderful gift to be able to determine ourselves by our own choice, and, in some sense, to frame our own destiny. They add that God can make evil serve good, and give a value to pain. Pain would only be irrational and an absolute evil if it had no value, if it was neither the expiation of a fault, nor the condition of a greater good.

Yet all this sounds rather like special pleading. Even though these remarks can refute pessimism (according to which the world is radically evil, and evil consists in the very fact of existence), they do not reply to all our questions, and do not comfort our pain. We feel instinctively that this is not all and that we must go further, that there is more to see and to know. "That is to say", writes P. Teilhard de Chardin, "is it quite sure if our minds are open to a light other than that of pure science, that we shall not find that the quantity and malice of evil here and now spread throughout the world do not show a certain *excess*, inexplicable to reason", if to the normal effects of the world process, "we do not add the extraordinary effect of some primordial catastrophe or failure?"[1] Here Christian faith gives us an answer, since it reveals the mystery of original sin, which is, says Pascal, "the mystery most obscure to our understanding", and that without which "we can have no knowledge of ourselves", for "our present condition has been so moulded in this abyss that man is more inconceivable without this mystery than this mystery is inconceivable to man".

This, however, takes us out of the sphere of natural reason. All that natural reason lets us say about the problem of evil is that we are too limited to be able to fathom the designs of providence. But it is enough for us that there is a providence, and that it watches over us as a mother over her children. We must not complain against God about something of which we know so little, but about which we do know that God's goodness, if we could grasp it in its height and breadth and depth, would dazzle our eyes with a brightness free from all shadow. From this point of view we conclude with Maurice Blondel: "the objections, the scandals,

---

[1] P. Teilhard de Chardin, *op. cit.*, p. 347. He seems to be referring especially to the revolt of the "Prince of this world", but what he says applies also to the sin of Adam.

are dispersed which trouble minds more generous than they are clear-sighted, or docile to the suggestions of love. Here again what seems dreadful is transformed, if we can understand and love, into a fresh reason for wonder and thanksgiving. How important it is, in order to forestall prejudice and bitterness, to offer this explanation of God's ways, and to bring souls to bow down before the unveiled sun, as Plato tells us in his account of the myth of Boreas. The pilgrim, in face of the efforts of the bitter wind to snatch from him the mantle of reasoning and reproaches with which he covers himself amid the tempests of the world, himself throws off all the coverings; these are no real protection when the warm rays of the sun and of love have penetrated through to his ignorance."[1]

[1] M. Blondel, *Exigences philosophiques du christianisme* (Paris, Presses Universitaires de France, 1950), pp. 245-6.

CONCLUSION

The fact must not be disguised that all these arguments in connection with the existence and nature of God remain inadequate to translate and render explicit in conceptual terms, as they try to do, our deep human experience. They have no chance of convincing except in so far as they awaken or re-awaken in us the sense of a creative and vivifying presence. It is not that they have no validity in themselves and by themselves, in the most rigorous sense. But the proof which they embody is not of the sensible order; if left to itself it only touches the reason, and is concerned with abstractions. It makes us think that God, as affirmed at the conclusion of the argument, is, so to speak, external both to the man who argues, and to the argument itself. It is a conception of this kind, one that is radically false, which is sometimes suggested by the expression "problem of God". God, if we speak accurately, is not a problem, but, in the sense put so plainly by Gabriel Marcel, a "mystery". For God is the meaning and reason of everything, while it is we and the world who are problems. The "problem of God" is nothing but our problem. If we do not take into account this aspect of the proof of God, which is entirely unique in its nature, as Anselm and Descartes maintained, we shall understand neither its meaning and essential form, nor the resistance it encounters, nor the fact of atheism which we cannot escape and which has to be explained. Hence we must return again to the knowledge of God in order to try to define more exactly its form and its most general conditions.

I. *THE PROOF OF GOD*

1. *Belief.* We usually speak of belief in God, not knowledge of God. This is an accurate way of speaking, since the word "belief" implies essentially the active adhesion to the object affirmed, or, if you like, the reflective repetition of the affirmation, the act by which the mind formulates to itself its adhesion to an assertion. We can say that belief, in this sense, amounts to assent. Now this assent is required wherever the assertion can suffer any element of uncertainty or doubt in the man who affirms it—or meet with any dispute on the part of the man to whom it is addressed. The assent or belief shows that a choice must be made between affirmation and denial, yes and no.

Thus belief in its strict sense implies a possibility of doubt. When this possibility is bound up with assertion, as may happen because assertion involves risk of error if not sufficiently well founded from the point of view of experience or reason, and when this risk is recognized by the man who formulates the assertion, we speak of opinion rather than of belief. On the other hand, when the assertion is concerned with facts or realities not of the sensible order (historical, metaphysical, moral, religious), we speak properly of belief. In that case we cannot say that the assent necessarily lacks certitude, but must say either that there is no intrinsic evidence for what is asserted (as in the case of the assent of supernatural faith, which is based, not on the evidence of its object, which is absolutely beyond reason, but on the extrinsic motives of credibility), or else that what is asserted, being complex of itself and requiring elaborate demonstration, can be disputed by others, either through lack of information or of exact reasoning, or else through lack of the necessary moral dispositions. Hence the possibility of doubt which accompanies belief is derived from the subjective conditions of the affirmation, rather than from what is affirmed, which may of itself possess the firmest objective validity. This is not so with opinion.

2. *Belief in God*. Thus we see that the affirmation of God depends primarily on belief, while this belief of itself involves a certitude which can be compared to no other, since it includes and supports all other certitudes. These are the two aspects of the proof of God which can account both for the resistance it encounters in many minds, which fail to realize its deep meaning, and also for the disquiet which it can cause in those who seek elsewhere for a ground for their certitude.

The mistake may be made here of supposing that what gives validity to the proofs of God is their conceptual and logical form, whereas they rest rather on the need for the absolute, and on the urge of the spirit. Edouard Le Roy has rightly insisted on this in recent times, but the weak point of his argument is, as we have seen, that he denies the validity of the explicit proof or of the logical reasoning, and hence that he *separates* the proof from its basis, from that urge of the spirit which dwells in it and animates it, as the soul in the body. In fact the truth about God is lived before it is known. The proofs do not cause it; it causes the proofs, which are only means for its expression and its justification after reflection. Here especially spontaneous use of reason is the chief source of all reflection. As with all belief, the proofs of God reinforce the affirmation. Hence it is that, being separated by abstraction from the living experience which they imply, they appear cold and dry, infinitely inadequate to express their true richness, and that they easily seem a conceptual game.

3. *The presence of God*. This living experience is that of the presence of God in everything that exists, and especially in the spiritual and moral life. For God is present everywhere, in the light of day, in the darkness of the star-lit night, in the colour and scent of the rose, in the movement of the stars, in the happy smile of a human being, in the courage to bear pain, in the rhythm of our hearts. Without argument,

but only from a natural impulse, the soul perceives in all this the presence of God, that is to say, grasps in a flash its inability to explain anything apart from God. All these arguments which I have laboured to develop are contained in this intuition of the "heart" or the "feeling" (to use Pascal's terms) which in essence is reason, the intuition here being only a mass of rapid judgements which seem instantaneous. It is this which really contains and supports all our reasoning, so that it is rather a matter of uncovering God than of proving him. We only "prove" what is absent; the presence, which at first is veiled or disguised, is uncovered. Or, to be more precise, it is God himself who uncovers himself or reveals himself to the soul which seeks him.

In fact, the movement towards God is as natural as our breathing; it can be called without exaggeration the breathing of the soul. In this sense it is quite true that we have an instinct for God, and that he is the most fundamental of our instincts, since he is nothing else than that very reason which constitutes us human beings. If all the reasons of things and of the world are in some way, as St Thomas holds, implanted and innate in our reason through its participation in that of the divine Thought, the one absolute Reason of everything must be the deepest, most essential and most spontaneous of our certitudes—so much so that our reason only finds itself and recognizes itself in discovering and recognizing absolute Reason. Thus we must accept what Pascal says, that we should not seek God nor attempt to prove him, if we had not already found him.

Nevertheless, this presence which reveals itself to us, and which the proofs strive to make manifest to the reasoning mind, is not presented to us as things experienced are presented. It is a spiritual presence, or even, more exactly, a demand upon the intelligence written upon everything that is, and which implies God as its only adequate meaning. Now a spiritual presence can only be grasped by the spirit. It follows from this that, when the spiritual element in us grows weak, the presence of God loses its evidence and vividness. God disappears from our horizon; he seems to dwell no longer in our world, and no longer to give life to our temporal existence. The proofs no longer prove anything, or seem not to do so, because the spring which moves them is broken. Thus Le Senne could say that "the discovery of God must unite an element of evidence and an element of faith". This is not only because God infinitely exceeds all the ideas we can form about him, but also because our knowledge of him is an uncovering. Our knowledge of him presupposes that at first he is hidden and mysterious, and, when achieved, it realizes that it is never finished, and that the discovery of God is never-ending. The noise of the world, worldly success, our passions and our interests, keep the thought of God at a distance, and at these moments of weakness or inattention it is to us as though God were no longer present everywhere. Then, as Pascal said against Descartes, certitude must attach itself to the memory, but the presence of God is neither felt nor lived, it becomes an idea and a concept. Or else it vanishes, as the world vanishes when we close our eyes. If it is true, as Claudel says, echoing Scripture, that "the world carries the signature of God", it is a signature which must be deciphered, and the meaning of which, clear to whoever wishes to grasp it, leads us to sheer mystery.

4. *The controversial nature of the proof of God.* The proofs for God cannot provide evidence; they presuppose it, and utilize it in various ways, and, when it is lacking, they do not fill the gap. For God does not come at the end of a process of reasoning, but at the beginning, and is embodied in it. That is why the proofs in some sense involve a struggle, and this from two points of view. First, as arguments, they supply a need of the reason. Though the intuition of which I have spoken is in itself clear and persuasive, our discursive reason has to turn it into precise concepts in order to get a proper grasp of it. It is a dispute between the *animus* and the *anima*, the heart and the reason, the spirit of the artist and that of

the mathematician. This inward struggle is both an aspect of our trial and a condition of our progress, for the continuous ebb and flow from one to the other, from "heart" to "reason", and from "reason" to "heart", gives fresh life to our reasons for belief, and enriches them with a force without which they would be a scaffolding with no building behind it. The proofs, in this aspect, are critical reflection, and, if you like, verification. They aim at convincing that part of me which depends on reasoning, but they also seek for a deepening of belief and a purification of thought. Faith seeks understanding. Belief, by means of the proofs, seeks to add light to heat.

Secondly, the proofs answer possible difficulties which are bound up with belief, since they support it. From this point of view they are worked out in order to convince the unbeliever, in order to give light and to clear away obstacles, and finally to lead the spirit and the heart of those to whom they are addressed to that inward region where they give all the nourishment of power and clarity which they possess.

Therefore we must make use of the proofs, but always in connection with the demand for understanding which is expressed in us by our need for the absolute, and which is their spring and their soul. If separated from this intuition and not used to explain it the proofs remain ineffective, and even run the risk of making God an *object*, which we suppose we can capture by force, through syllogism and demonstration, just like objects in the world. Belief cannot change itself into algebra, and get rid of the element of faith it carries with it.

II. ATHEISM

1. *The problem of atheism.* To the believer atheism is a mystery, while to the atheist belief is a mystery. We must try to understand both.

Those who feel deeply the overwhelming power and evidential value of the proof of God are liable to misunderstand the reasoning of the atheist, and hence to confirm him in his unbelief. I am speaking here, of course, not of a practical atheism which is only an unsuspected and deceptive materialism, but of an atheism which in good faith tries to justify itself and reject the proofs. Now usually the mistake of the atheist lies in asking for a proof which is compelling, in the same way that the rules of arithmetic compel us to agree that two and two make four, that the earth goes round the sun, or the sum of the angles of a triangle is equal to two right angles. In one sense God is more certain than all these compelling truths, but it is in a different way, and the atheist does not usually grasp the difference. If you try to overpower him by force of argument it only fixes him more firmly in his denial, or his inability to discover God, for argument, by definition, cannot give him what he wants. If we build everything upon the proof and its logical force, we open the door to doubt and scepticism. As Pascal saw, all metaphysical reasoning, even when the conclusion is reached, leaves a fear that we may be deceived, or at least that we may not have examined everything. Moreover, if we make God an object reached as a conclusion, we change God into a concept which, being separated from the source which gives it its true meaning, fails to carry conviction, even though it may leave an opponent silenced. Then the resistance of the atheist appears to the believer, who trusts too much to his abstract logic, as a sign of bad faith and deliberate refusal to understand. Discussion becomes impossible, and communication is broken off.

It is quite true that the atheist often lays himself open to this misunderstanding, for he desires and calls for a power of conviction which shall dispense him from making any effort. Yet Pascal says of the God of Abraham, Isaac and Jacob, that "we only seek him with groans", that is, by a complete and painful opening of the soul and a profound humility, and this already applies to the discovery of the God "of philosophers and scholars". He only reveals himself to the poor in spirit; he is a presence more than a reason, and a gift more than a conquest. The positivist spirit is sometimes a great obstacle here, for, contrary to what we might suppose, it lacks the sense of the concrete and of the living, and when it demands rigour, as would be quite correct in other circumstances, it thinks of abstract rigour to which it is accustomed. For the positivist the plan is simply the same as the house, and the blueprint the same as the reality. He forgets that, even though the plan and the blueprint are true, they are only so as symbols. Now, when we are concerned with God, the proof must be ballasted with a spiritual experience, or adapted to that demand for the absolute which gives it its meaning. Thus there is no lack of positivity; here it is even more perfect than in experimental knowledge. But it is of a different order because it embraces and appeals, not to pure abstract reason, but to the whole man.

All this explains how it is both possible and impossible to deny God. Atheism has to be possible, in order that the knowledge of God may have a moral value. If God could be seen in the same way that we see two and two make four, freedom of assent and its value would disappear. Belief in God must overcome many obstacles, such as the density of the sensible world, pain, evil and death; it is also a sort of scandal to minds unfitted for metaphysics that the universe should *seem* not to need God. It is not necessary that there should be sensible evidence for God's existence, that the truth about God should have the solidity, the overwhelming character of a physical fact. But from another point of view it must be impossible to deny God; the evidence, lost on the level of fact, must be recovered through an infinitely higher kind of power, on the level of total experience, at once and indivisibly rational, affective and moral.

This evidence, as we have seen, strictly speaking is that which is bound up with the absolute condition of intelligibility of all that exists, in the moral world and in the universe of things. Without God there can be nothing, and everything becomes irrational. All the proofs together say nothing else, borrowing from this basic evidence their light and force. But it is right and necessary that this evidence itself should be verified, so to speak, *from within*. It carries in itself its own light. The mistake of the atheist does not lie in wishing to criticize the evidence, but in making it something external. Now, whether we like it or not, we are within it and all proof is worked out within it, precisely because God encompasses us, and we can never find him unless we return to ourselves. "Return to thyself", says St Augustine, "it is there that truth dwells."

2. *The meaning of atheism*. It remains that atheism must have some *appearance* of truth, the appearance here being the obstacle that must be surmounted if we are to discover the presence of God, just as error makes scepticism seem acceptable. This appearance must be seen through if we wish to give a firm foundation to the validity of reason. We may go so far as to say that, from one point of view, we should see an element of truth in atheism. For it is true that the atheist is only rejecting an indefensible conception of God, and that his denial of an idolatrous notion of God is really a genuine affirmation of the true God. As de Lubac puts it so well, the more we believe in God, the more we are atheists as to false gods. Further, we must always keep in mind how insufficient and inadequate to express the infinite and incomprehensible reality of God is our conception of it, however carefully elaborated. From this point of view, atheism, to the believer, is only a form of that negative way by which the greatest thinkers of Christianity have approached belief in God. Thus atheism can in certain cases help us to reach a more vivid awareness of the inexhaustible demands of a valid idea of God. Not only from a motive of charity, but also to employ to the full the element of truth involved in atheism, we should make use of atheism itself to purify still further and to spiritualize our belief in God, and at the same time to help the atheist who seeks with so much labour to recover

belief in God. Though he does not see it clearly, God is found in the negation of his thoughts.

Above all we should realize that we can only argue effectively with the atheist, if we show ourselves as witnesses, that is, as witnesses of an experience lived on two levels, the rational level of intelligibility, and the practical level of spiritual efficacy. We are too ready in this matter to trust entirely to abstract reasoning, forgetting that sometimes a wealth of discourse is more in paper than solid coin. Often indeed silence is more fruitful in trust and persuasion than logic, however well constructed. The atheist, in face of obstacles which are more affective than rational, is attentive rather to the life of the believer than to his arguments. Moreover, these depend not so much on their conceptual content as on their spiritual meaning. Not that the conceptual content is unimportant; far from it, as I have been at pains to show. But it is in some degree subordinate, and hence, though sometimes defective and complicated in its technical form, it can be animated with such a spirit, it can possess such power, that it only acts as a springboard for reaching the transcendent (as Kierkegaard and Jaspers say), being left behind at the very moment when it is used.

3. *Systematic atheism*. Everyone, says St Thomas, has a natural knowledge of God. But we must also know him and discover him *as God*. So, too, I perceive myself necessarily and in all my acts, because I am constantly present to myself, though reflection is needed to make this presence actual. I know myself from the very fact that I live; I only recognize myself by recollection. Men are given more to being polytheists than atheists. They fashion gods in their own image, and then desire to make use of them. After that they deny all the gods made by their hands, and think they have established the nothingness of God. "Man punishes himself for finding his way blocked by committing suicide", says Le Senne. Contemporary thought provides many examples of this pseudo-conversion to nothingness, when a man discovers

that he has been deceived twice over, in not grasping God as a thing, and in finding in the idea of God phantasms which are parasites upon it, and demolish it. Yet the labour undergone, and, as it were, the bitterness and resentment accompanying the conclusion, do not fail to witness in their own way to the existence of the true God. For if absence is, here again, a kind of presence, it is in vain that atheists of our time wish to try and reach a point at which absence itself would vanish in the complete disappearance of all questions about anything. "You see this emptiness above our heads?" asks Goetz of Heinrich. "It is God. . . . Silence is God; absence is God."[1] The attempt, however, is foiled in advance. For by this very act man destroys himself hopelessly. If God is lost, man is lost. But above all silence and absence speak more loudly and clearly than any argument; the emptiness of the world without God is itself filled with God. Like that fabulous animal which the ancients called "catoblepas", and which devoured its own feet without knowing it, systematic atheists in our time suffer the double shame of annihilating themselves by their negation, and of invoking God by their refusal.

Kierkegaard says again and again that man is only man "before God". In face of God, in the act of belief or of adoration, he knows himself in his wretchedness and his greatness. He knows that his nobility consists in witnessing to God, from whom he receives all he is and all he has, and especially that consciousness by which God expresses himself in him. When Sartre, through the voice of Goetz and in the passage quoted above, cries, "I have decided myself about evil; I have invented good myself", he is trying to describe that "wonderful game", the kind of fright that children give themselves by imagining ghosts and phantoms. And, in order to assure himself that he has no fear, he begins to whistle and sing, like the traveller lost at night in the forest, who wishes to give himself courage: "Joy, tears of joy! Alleluia. . . . I am

[1] J. P. Sartre, *Le Diable et le bon Dieu*, Xe tableau.

setting us free. No more heaven, no more hell: only the earth."

So he can still make an idol of nothingness, but man is devoured by this nothingness which has become God. Kierkegaard and Dostoievski have given magnificent descriptions of this vertigo of nothingness, and we must admit that it is one of the experiences of our time. Yet it does not so far seem to have yielded any other fruit than scepticism and amorality. Everything can be certain to the atheist, except that there is certainty. All our knowledge and all our values float in a void: reality becomes that of a dream, almost a nightmare. Zarathustra is drunk with his own words, without even knowing if they make sense.

4. *The "crisis of God"*. In the words of Le Senne, we find that "God is at a crisis". He is so in many ways. In our thought which, as we have seen, is false to him through its inability to conceive him in his infinity. In evil and in pain, which raise problems in our hearts. In history, which denies him by injustice and wickedness. In our lives, which witness against him by our sins. But this "crisis of God" cannot serve as an alibi for us. For God does not go bail for our idleness and hypocrisy. It is not his business simply to reassure us; he is our consolation, but also our goad. He is for us both peace and war, light and darkness, tranquillity and anxiety, life and death, present and absent, close at hand and far away. He includes all contradictions, since he resolves them all. The apparent strength of atheism is that it grasps the negative; its obvious weakness is that it grasps nothing else. But our unhappiness, individual and collective, lies in surrendering to the negative and helping atheism to establish itself there. Our unhappiness lies, too, in failing to understand that, as Christ, in the teaching of Pascal and of the Christian faith, "is in agony until the end of time", so too, on the plane of natural reason, God is always "at a crisis", in the sense that belief in God must always be won again, at every moment of our existence, and at every period of human history, in spite of

the obstacles which it encounters, of the scandals which it raises, and, in general, in spite of all the negation which accompanies it in our finite state.

Pascal is right in saying that it is never enough either to have grasped the proofs of God, nor to have demonstrated them, since we must still "show how it is good to believe in him", and that belief in God ought to transform our whole life. Le Senne writes that for him "the main proof for the existence of God is the joy he finds in the thought that God exists". Nothing can be truer or more profound. God gives unity both to our thought and to our life; he asserts himself in the harmony he brings about. He reconciles us with ourselves, with our neighbour and with the world. But this joy and this harmony are never given once for all. They only blossom through effort and generosity, suffering and humility. They call for an opening of the spirit which must be reclosed every day. Belief involves labour and strife.

Yet, under this very aspect, when God is acknowledged and believed, he inspires witness of unlimited fruitfulness in the midst of the world. The idea of God, when all its requirements are understood, is the most powerful there is, since all depends upon it. The believer who lives deeply his faith in God, feels himself seized in its grip and knows no rest. The idea of God prevents us from ever being satisfied with any finite truth, or setting our heart on any good fortune, or finding our peace in any human justice. The whole movement of history, its tumults and its strife, is rooted in this belief in God, who gives it its deepest meaning.

To dream of an idea of God which does not involve struggle, and is freed from all that is negative, is to lose the whole spiritual content of the freedom by which man works out his own destiny. We must make choice of God, and choose ourselves by choosing him, for it is by this choice that we decide whether to be simply a thing or to be a person. Basically we are concerned with the idea of God alone. Everything else is a mere game. The idea of God is the very form of our freedom and of our responsibility. Hence it is a mistake to turn the movement towards God into an escape. On the contrary this movement always takes us back to ourselves and to the world, so that pain and danger may lead us to accept all its unhappiness and moral wealth. The idea of God lays upon our shoulders the burden of the world and of history.

However, we must confess that we could not say all this, at least with certainty, unless our knowledge of God, as given by reason, were not contained, so to speak, in what the Christian revelation teaches us about the mystery of God. The mere idea of God which pure deism offers us would cause no crisis, if it did not appear to introduce us to a higher and more perfect knowledge, infinitely more important to us, because it teaches us that we are part of a supernatural plan which makes us, in a sense beyond the conception of reason, children of God. In discussions about what is called the "problem of God" it is almost always more or less Christianity which is at stake.

Hence it is that this problem takes on quite a new gravity and urgency. Yet it keeps its fundamental meaning, since the whole majestic edifice of revelation implies basically the rational knowledge of God. If through the fact of revelation, when we make choice of God, we thereby choose what is immeasurably beyond reason, reason is still involved in this choice, which presupposes that we must make use of its light. Faith does not get rid of this: on the contrary it adds to it and consecrates it in its own order. Thus there is brought about a kind of unity of the revelation of reason and of the revelation of the Man-God, who gives to the former the fullness of its meaning. After this all holds together: reason which is the ground plan of faith finds in faith a light which it cannot ever guess at, but is bound to welcome, in all humility, as the most splendid gift and the most wonderful perfection.

SELECT BIBLIOGRAPHY

*Works by non-Catholics

DANIÉLOU, Jean, S.J., *God and Us*, London, Mowbrays, 1957, or *God and the Ways of Knowing*, New York, Meridian Books, 1956.

*FARRER, *Austin, Finite and Infinite*, London, Dacre Press, and Naperville, Ill., Allenson, 1943.

GARRIGOU-LAGRANGE, *God, His Existence and His Nature*, 2 Vols., Herder, 1936.

GILSON, Etienne, *God in Philosophy*, New Haven, Conn., Yale, 1941.

HAWKINS, D. J. B., *Essentials of Theism*, London, 1949, New York, 1950, Sheed and Ward.

LUBAC, Henri de, S.J., *The Drama of Atheistic Humanism*, London and New York, Sheed and Ward, 1953.

MARITAIN, Jacques, *Approaches to God*, New York, Harper, 1954.

*MASCALL, E. L., *He Who Is, a Study in Traditional Theism*, London and New York, Longmans, 1943.

PONTIFEX, Dom Mark, *The Existence of God*, London and New York, Longmans, 1947.

PONTIFEX, Dom Mark, and TRETHOWAN, Dom Illtyd, *The Meaning of Existence*, London and New York, 1953.